The Ro
Eu

Written and researched by
Peterjon Cresswell, Dan Goldstein and Simon Evans

Edited by
Dan Goldstein

ROUGH
GUIDES

Commissioning editor: Jonathan Buckley
Editor: Dan Goldstein
Design and layout: Dan Goldstein
Production: Helen Ostick, Susanne Hillen, Michelle Draycott, Henry Iles
Rough Guide Series editor: Mark Ellingham
Photography: Empics, Nottingham, England

....

The editor would like to thank Danny Feys, Tony Jones, Mark Harris, Bob & Ulrich, Mike Hammond, Colin Panter at Empics and Jan Purath

Published May 2000 by Rough Guides Ltd, 62–70 Shorts Gardens, London WC2H 9AB.

Distributed by the Penguin Group:
Penguin BooksLtd, 27 Wrights Lane, London W8 5TZ
Penguin Books USA Inc., 375 Hudson Street, New York 10014, USA
Penguin Books Australia Ltd, 487 Maroondah Highway, PO Box 257, Ringwood, Victoria
   3134, Australia
Penguin Books Canada Ltd, 10 Alcorn Avenue, Toronto, Ontario, Canada M4V 1E4
Penguin Books (NZ) Ltd, 182–190 Wairau Road, Auckland 10, New Zealand
Printed by Caledonian
96pp
A catalogue record for this book is available from the British Library.
ISBN 1-85828-669-7

....

The publisher and authors have done their best to ensure the accuracy and currency of the information in The Rough Guide to Euro 2000, however they can accept no responsibility for any loss, injury, or inconvenience sustained by any traveller as a result of information or advice contained in the guide.

CONTENTS

INTRODUCTION

Between Saturday 10 June and Sunday 2 July, a major landmark will be reached in the evolution of European football. Not just the first European Championship of a new century and a new millennium, but the first tournament of its kind to be jointly hosted by two countries.

When UEFA awarded the Euro 2000 finals to Belgium and Holland in 1995, the move was seen as a calculated gamble. Neither country was large enough to host the competition on its own, but between them the Belgian and Dutch FAs made a compelling case for co-hosting. The two nations have more in common than merely being geographical next-door neighbours, with a shared social and political heritage dating back to before the formation of the European Community. The local transport infrastructure, both within each country and between the two, is one of Europe's most complete. And both nations have a reputation for cool, calm efficiency – an essential pre-requisite for any country contemplating the staging of an event as big as this, let alone two states wishing to share its administration between them.

Even so, there are those who question the wisdom of two distinct bodies being entrusted with the organisation of a tournament such as Euro 2000. After all, organisers inevitably bicker among themselves – surely co-hosting is merely a recipe for more disagreements? Similarly, breakdowns in communication seem certain to multiply if there are two languages involved. And no matter how good the transport links, it will surely never be as easy for teams, officials, media and fans to travel from one country to another, as it is to move within one? (This point has been highlighted by the decision to stiffen border controls between Holland and Belgium temporarily during Euro 2000, as an anti-hooligan measure.)

These questions will be answered this summer, along with the more usual pre-competition issues, such as who'll win the thing? Will the football be any good? And will it be possible to buy a portion of chips without mayonnaise dripping all over them?

It is these issues that this *Rough Guide* has been designed to address, providing a complete yet accessible companion to Euro 2000, both for fans travelling to the Low Countries, and for those planning to watch the whole event from the comfort of their sofa. Have a good one.

THE ESSENTIALS

Regardless of the merits of two countries trying to host the event between them, there's no denying that Euro 2000 is easily accessible from Britain. With frequent flights to Brussels and Amsterdam, a choice of ferry crossings from Dover, and the option of taking either Eurostar (for foot passengers) or Le Shuttle (for those wishing to take their own cars), there's no excuse not to make the effort. If you can get a ticket, you ought to get over. And if you get over, it will help to go armed with some basic information on the two host nations…

Basics – Belgium

If Belgian football is a game of two halves, Belgian society is a culture of **two tongues**. **French** is the language of Brussels and Wallonia, **Flemish** (Dutch, basically) that of Flanders. Speaking French to a Bruges barman is like adopting a plummy, shire counties accent to a Glaswegian. In Flanders, if in doubt – speak English.

EU nationals and those of the US, Canada, Australia and New Zealand require only a **passport** to enter the country.

The currency is the **Belgian franc** (BF), divided into 100 centimes. There are about 60BF to £1. There are coins for 50 centimes, 1, 5, 20 and 50BF. Notes come in denominations of 100, 200, 500, 1,000, 2,000, 5,000 and 10,000BF. Keep a supply of 20BF coins ready for using the toilet in bars and restaurants. You may be given Luxembourg francs in your change – they are legal but unpopular tender here. Banks are the best places to **change money**, open Mon–Fri 9am–noon & 2–4pm. They charge a 450BF fee for cashing Eurocheques. Note that **credit-card payment** is not as commonplace as elsewhere in Western Europe.

From outside the country, the **telephone code** for Belgium is 32 – for Brussels add a 2, for Liège 4, for Bruges 50 and for Charleroi 71. Belgian coin phones take 5, 20 or 50BF pieces, but you can only direct-dial internationally from phones marked with European flags – the access code is 00. Standard *Belgacom* **phonecards** are available from post offices and newsstands (200BF for 20 units, 1,000BF for 105). Cheap international rates are in operation 8pm–8am and all day Sundays and holidays.

Train travel in Belgium is quick, reliable and cheap at 300BF for a 100km journey. You'll get 40% discount off return tickets from Friday evening to Sunday evening. **Buses** are generally used for short distances in and around towns – bus stations are almost always next-door to the train variety. **Brussels Taxistop** (☎02/223 2231, fax 02/223 2232, open Mon–Fri 10.30am–6pm) is a shared lift service for Belgium and Europe, charging 200BF plus 1.30BF per km.

Hotel accommodation in Belgium is expensive – minimum 1,000BF for a double room. The *Tourism Centre* in Brussels, Rue Marché aux Herbes 63 (open daily 9am–7pm, ☎02/504 0390, fax 02/504 0270) can make free hotel reservations anywhere in Belgium except Brussels. *Bed & Brussels*, Rue Victor Greyson 58 (☎02/646 0737, fax 02/644 01 14, open Mon–Fri 9am–6pm) can book you a room anywhere in Belgium. Leave your details on their answerphone.

Food is more important to the Belgians than it is to the Dutch, although the northern half of the country serves up plainer stuff than the French-influenced south. Buckets of **steamed mussels** in various sauces are a staple diet everywhere. A **main course** will be around 500BF, but look out for *plats du jour* at perhaps 300BF. If you're on a budget, Belgium is the **home of the chip**, and proud of it.

If Belgians took their football as seriously as they do their **beer**, no other team would be getting a look-in at Euro 2000. A glass of standard **lager** – ordered as a *pintje/chope* – will probably be Stella, Maes or Jupiler, and weigh in at 40–50BF. For around twice this, you can usually order any of at least 20 **speciality beers**, often many more. These may be fruit-flavoured; Trappist (such as Chimay, which comes in three different strengths); or *lambic* (aired and matured in production). Wheat beer (*wit-bier/bière blanche*) is a refreshing option, often served with a slice of lemon. Belgian bar **opening hours** are generous, and clubbing is not nearly as popular as pubbing.

Basics – Holland

EU citizens and those of the USA, Canada, Australia and New Zealand require only a **passport** to enter the Netherlands.

The Dutch **currency** is the guilder, abbreviated to f, divided into 100 cents. There are coins for 5c, 10c, 25c, f1, f2.50 and f5, and notes for f10, f25, f50, f100, f250 and f1,000. There are around f3.3 to £1. Banks offer the best **exchange rates**, and are open Mon–Fri 9am–4pm, with occasional late Thursday opening in the main cities. *GWK* offices are open much later, and can give cash advances on credit cards. Payment by credit card is widespread.

Phonecards, in f5, f10 and f25 sizes, are sold at post offices and tourist information (*VVV*) offices. From outside the country, the code for Holland is 31; for Amsterdam add 20, Rotterdam 10, Eindhoven 40 and Arnhem 26. Add a 0 before the city code if you're calling inland. From inside Holland, the international access code is 00, and the reduced rate period for European calls is Mon–Fri 8pm–8am, all day Sat–Sun.

Holland is a small country and few **journeys** take more than three hours. **Trains** are comfortable and efficient, and fares, calculated by the kilometre, are reasonable. A journey of 50km costs around f15, with a 10% discount on return fares if you come back the same day on a *dagretour*. Buying a ticket onboard incurs a hefty supplement.

Bus stations are nearly always located next to train termini, and local services are equally cheap and efficient. Like all public transport in Holland, buses run on the *Nationale Strippenkaart* system, in which a ticket strip is divided into numbered bars, which the bus driver then stamps according to the length of your journey. Simply tell him your destination

Useful contacts

For ticket enquiries (confirmed ticket-holders only)
Euro 2000 Foundation, PO Box 70028, 3000 LK Rotterdam, Holland

For official accommodation enquiries
Euro 2000 Accommodation Agency, Lakenblekerstraat 49, 1431 GE Aalsmeer, Holland
☎ +31 (0)20 200 1234, fax +31 (0)297 388 001, email info@e2000aa.nl

Tourist offices in the UK
Belgium – Premier House, 2 Gayton Road, Harrow, Middx, HA1 2XU
Holland – PO Box 523, London, SW1E 6NT

when you board. On **city trams** and **metros**, it's up to you to stamp the ticket in the machine by folding the strip to include sufficient bars. Few urban journeys require more than two. The driver can sell you strips of two, three or eight bars onboard; more economical 15-bar (f11.75) and 45-bar (f34.50) strips are sold at train stations and newsstands.

For all the efficiency of the transport, **cycling** is often the best way to get around. There are bike hire offices at most train stations; they charge about f10 a day, but require a form of ID and f200 deposit. Be sure to use a sturdy lock wherever you park.

Hotels in Holland are not particularly cheap but there is a **national reservation service**, *Nederlands Reserverings Centrum* (open Mon–Fri 8am–8pm, Sat 8am–2pm, ☎070/419 5500, fax 070/419 5519), charging a f5 booking fee.

Large towns have a *VVV* tourist office at or near the train station, where you can book a room for f5 commission per person. In a two-star hotel, expect to pay around f100–130 for a double room with a bath/shower. Pensions are about f50 per person, youth hostels f30. Don't be too surprised if room rates rise dramatically during Euro 2000.

Useful words and phrases

English	Dutch/Flemish	French
Yes	*Ja*	*Oui*
No	*Nee*	*Non*
Two beers, please	*Twee bier alstublieft*	*Deux demis, s'il vous plaît*
Thank you	*Dank u*	*Merci*
Hello	*Hallo*	*Bonjour*
Goodbye	*Tot ziens*	*Au revoir*
Do you speak English?	*Spreekt u Engels?*	*Vous parlez anglais?*
Men's	*Mannen*	*Hommes*
Women's	*Vrouwen*	*Dames*
Where is the stadium?	*Hoe kom ik in het stadion?*	*Où est le stade?*
What's the score?	*Wat is de stand?*	*Où en sommes-nous?*
Referee	*Scheidsrechter*	*L'arbitre*
Offside	*Buitenspel*	*Hors jeu*

Dutch **cooking** is high on protein, low on variety, relying on fish, meat and dairy produce. *Eetcafés* provide a good-value version of it – look out for the *dagschotel*, the dish of the day, at around f20, or three-course tourist menus at f25–30. The Dutch tend to dine early, so restaurants normally only stay open until 11pm. Most towns have a fair ethnic selection, especially Chinese, Surinamese and Indonesian. Restaurant bills are subject to a 17.5% tax surcharge and 15% service charge.

The traditional Dutch bar is the *bruine kroeg*, or **brown café**, cosy and tobacco-stained. These places serve food until early evening and lager (*pils*) in small glasses with a large head theatrically skimmed off by a plastic knife. Heineken, Amstel, Oranjeboom and Grolsch are the most common brews, but more adventurous Belgian varieties should also be available. The national spirit is *jenever*, a gin made from molasses and juniper berries. Most bars stay open until 1am, or 2am at weekends.

Note that the renowned liberal attitude to **smoking marijuana** in Holland applies only to designated **coffee shops**.

Ticketing

This is the third major football tournament to be staged in Europe in six years, and the organisers are keen to learn from both Euro '96 in England and France's hosting of the 1998 World Cup. In England, tickets were widely available to the public but inadequately advertised, resulting in a lot of empty seats at some group games. In France, too many seats were allocated to sponsors and tour operators, so that while every game was technically a sellout, many matches lacked atmosphere as fans of the participating teams were few in number.

Every game at Euro 2000 is technically a sellout, too, with all seats having been sold in advance in three tranches – two before the draw for the finals was made last December, and one afterwards. By comparison with France '98, however, far fewer tickets were allocated to the package-tour and corporate hospitality brigade, while more went to the national FAs of the teams taking part.

Prices were also reasonable (in many cases lower than at Euro '96), with a simple three-band system being applied. Each host stadium has three categories of seating, with prices varying according to the status of the fixture – group game, quarter-final and so forth.

If your order for match tickets has been confirmed, you should receive yours by recorded delivery during May. If they don't turn up, contact the Euro 2000 Foundation (only postal enquiries will be dealt with) at the address in the panel.

If you don't already have tickets, simply travelling to the tournament in the hope of getting them is probably more pointless at Euro 2000 than at any previous tournament. All tickets bear the name of the person who originally ordered them, and the authorities are promising stringent checks at security checkpoints around the grounds. And despite what you may have read about the Dutch government's failure to outlaw ticket-touting, the police in both countries are under instructions to clamp down hard – on buyers as well as sellers.

Last-minute changes

Organising an event like Euro 2000 is an ongoing process, and some logistical details had not yet been finalised when this book went to press. In particular, the pickup and departure points for shuttle buses to and from grounds, and the location of temporary car parks, were yet to be announced – if in doubt, check locally as soon as you arrive.

Similarly, it may be that security concerns will persuade local police to allocate certain special trains or buses to supporters of one team only, rendering some of the transport details given here redundant.

Alcohol is also a moot point. Having a beer before, during and after the game is part of the everyday football experience in both Belgium and Holland, but the prospect of alcohol bans (inside and/or outside stadia) shouldn't be ruled out. If any such bans are applied, it will be at short notice, but don't expect local bar-owners to break the rules – it is literally more than their job's worth.

THE TEAMS: GROUP A

ENGLAND

"If the back door is all there is, then we'll be happy to go through it." That was how manager Kevin Keegan described his team's prospects as the Euro 2000 qualifiers entered their final phase and England, their fate in the hands of others, could only wait and hope that Sweden would do them a favour and deny Poland the point they needed to enter the play-offs. Sweden won, of course, letting England through precisely the back door Keegan had described. An unconvincing 2–1 win over Scotland followed, and the most unlikely of all Euro 2000's qualifying stories was complete.

Having been spared the ignominy of being the only major European power absent from this summer's festivities, England now have the chance to measure their progress against the best, in an event that is second only to the World Cup in international importance. Yet 'progress' is all most fans expect to see – the notion of, say, making the last four, as England did on home soil four years ago, seems as wild now as it did when the Swedes and the Poles took the field for that last group-stage qualifier back in November 1999.

After succeeding Glenn Hoddle midway through the qualifying campaign, Keegan has had little time in which to impose his ideas on the squad. There are signs that England's experiment with a 'continental' counter-attacking game, first espoused by Terry Venables and then refined by Hoddle, may be coming to an end – ironically at a time when the foreign influence on English football, at both playing and coaching levels, is greater than it's ever been.

Keegan's argument is that European opponents still fear a traditional English approach more than anything else. He may have a point – but exactly how much Europe has to fear is something that can't be quantified until June, when the England manager faces his first real test.

The pedigree
There's no other way of looking at it – England and the European Championship really don't get on. From Lancaster Gate's refusal to enter the first

competition in 1958 to Gareth Southgate's penalty miss at Wembley 38 years later, the story is essentially one of spurned opportunities.

When England qualified for the final stages for the first time in 1968, it was as champions of the world. More than that, Alf Ramsey's World Cup-winning squad was generally reckoned to have been improved as the qualifying tournament had gone on. But in their semi-final against Yugoslavia in Florence, England's grand plans were ripped apart. The low point of a bad-tempered game was Alan Mullery being sent off mid-way through the second half (the first England player ever to be suffer that fate in an international), after which Yugoslavia gradually took control. They won the game in the closing minutes, and Ramsey's men were left with the bittersweet consolation of a 2–0 victory over the Soviet Union in the third-place play-off.

There was more disappointment in 1972 – when England under-estimated West Germany's attacking ambitions in their quarter-final first leg at Wembley and were outplayed, 3–1 – and again four years later, when Don Revie's team failed even to get that far.

In 1980, an England side 'in transition' never really got started in the finals in Italy, beginning to play football only when it was too late – an enjoyable 2–1 win over Spain in the last group game was sadly irrelevant for both teams.

After another failure to qualify in 1984, England put on perhaps their worst-ever finals display in West Germany four years later, losing 1–0 to Ireland in their opening game, being played off the park by Holland in a 3–1 defeat, then apparently giving up altogether in another 3–1 loss, this time to the Soviet Union.

Spelling it out – Alan Shearer

It seemed as though things couldn't get any worse, but after the national morale boost of Italia '90, England went to Euro '92 under Graham Taylor and simply embarrassed themselves, drawing goallessly with Denmark and France before infamously losing 2–1 to Sweden.

And then came Euro '96, a welcome antidote to decades of under-achievement. As host nation, England played all their games at Wembley, and though the first was a disappointing 1–1 draw with Switzerland, Gazza's spectacular goal in a 2–0 win over the Scots and the 4–1 mauling of Holland that followed were enough to get an entire country behind Terry Venables' team. A slightly lucky win over Spain on penalties in the quarter-finals was followed by an extremely unlucky loss to Germany by the same means. It was a sad end, but a noble one…

The players

Though the squad bequeathed to manager **Kevin Keegan** was patently not up to the job, he has had precious little time in which to effect major changes, tending to concentrate on attitude, rather than personnel.

It all starts with Arsenal 'keeper **David Seaman**, seemingly certain to be preferred to the currently more dependable **Nigel Martyn** (Leeds), if only for his infinitely greater international experience. In front of Seaman, it's not yet clear whether Keegan will favour two or three central defenders – he may even chop and change during the tournament. Either way, the Arsenal duo of **Tony Adams** and **Martin Keown** are sure to be involved if fitness permits, as are **Sol Campbell** (Spurs), **Gareth Southgate** (Aston Villa) and **Rio Ferdinand** (West Ham).

Manchester United brothers **Gary** and **Philip Neville** will increase the options in both defence and midfield, with **Kieron Dyer** (Newcastle), **Jason Wilcox** (Leeds) and **Trevor Sinclair** (West Ham) all capable of filling wing-back roles if the manager decides he wants them. Arsenal's Ray Parlour and Chelsea's Dennis Wise are among the possibilities for the anchorman role, while creative duties inevitably fall at the feet of Old Trafford's **David Beckham** and **Paul Scholes**.

Upfront, captain **Alan Shearer** (Newcastle) seems to have hit form at exactly the right time to make an impression at his last international tournament, with supporting roles likely to come from Liverpool's **Michael Owen**, **Andy Cole** (Manchester Unitd) and **Emile Heskey** (Leicester).

GERMANY

Seldom have Germany, the most successful nation in the history of the European Championship and current holders of the title, approached the tournament's final stages in such a state of apparent disarray. The *National-Elf* qualified for Euro 2000 with an uncharacteristic stutter, losing away to Turkey and failing to beat the same opposition at home, and relying on results elsewhere to spare them the embarrassment of a play-off. Since then the team's preparations have been hampered by uncertain team selection, the poor form of key players and an increasingly impatient domestic media.

In many ways, the situation is comparable to that of England, the old enemy who the Germans must face not just at Euro 2000 but also in qualifying for the 2002 World Cup. Like the Premiership, the German *Bundesliga* is enjoying a period of unprecedented financial growth. Exotic imports from the far reaches of Eastern Europe, Latin America and Africa have flooded into the domestic game, depriving raw, homegrown talent of the first-team football it needs if it is to mature. At the same time, established international stars no longer feel the need to play abroad to earn big-money salaries. While this is convenient for management, who don't need to travel far to assess a player's form, it may yet have a negative impact on the national team's ability to vary its approach according to different opponents – an asset critical to Germany's victory at Euro '96.

As the game has got richer, so the balance of football power has shifted away from the German FA, the DFB, and into the hands of the clubs. Historically, domestic interests have always played second fiddle to those of the national side. Today, for the first time, the big clubs are openly questioning the usefulness of international football, planting the seeds of an ambivalence which has not yet reached the depths of that in, say, Spain or England, but which could easily get that way.

The pedigree

Though they may be more vividly remembered for their World Cup triumphs of 1954, 1974 and 1990, the Germans have often reserved their best football for the European Championship. After a false start in 1967, when

Not pretty, but effective – Carsten Jancker outjumps his man in qualifying

a goalless draw in Albania robbed them of a place in the final stages, a classic West German line-up including Franz Beckenbauer at sweeper, the unpredictable playmaker Gunter Netzer and *der Bomber* Gerd Müller upfront swept all before them in the 1972 event. England were the first to feel the force, losing 3–1 at Wembley in the quarter-finals as Netzer ran Alf Ramsey's tired side ragged. Müller then scored twice as Belgium were beaten 2–1 in Antwerp, and twice more as the Soviet Union were crushed 3–0 in the final in Brussels.

This team would go on to win the World Cup on home soil two years later, playing a brand of 'total football' every bit as attractive as that of the Holland side they beat in the final in Munich. In 1976, a hat-trick of international honours beckoned after Yugoslavia were beaten 4–2 in the European Championship semi-finals. In the final, however, West Germany were guilty of a certain arrogance, were outplayed by Czechoslovakia, and lost their trophy on penalties after a 2–2 draw – the only time the Germans have failed to win a shoot-out in top-level competitive football.

The brilliant Bernd Schuster, appearing in his only major finals, helped West Germany to regain their crown in Italy in 1980, but this was a poor tournament – and a poor team – by comparison with '76, the mood personified by the physical Hans-Peter Briegel and Horst Hrubesch, scorer of both goals in the final against Belgium in Rome.

In 1984, a rare late defensive lapse against Spain in Paris cost the Germans a place in the semi-finals, and four years later, despite hosting the tournament for the first time (and boasting a team including Lothar Matthäus, Jürgen Klinsmann and Rudi Völler among others), they were put in the shade by the victorious Dutch side of Gullit and van Basten.

After winning the World Cup in 1990, the squad was strengthened – on paper, at least – by the addition of players from the former East Germany, who joined to form a united German side following the fall of the Berlin Wall. Yet, having reached the final of Euro '92 in Sweden, the side capitulated in the face of Peter Schmeichel's goalkeeping and lost 2–0 to unfancied Denmark.

In England four years later, an ageing, less obviously creative side was further weakened by injuries, yet drew on the traditional German strengths of discipline and resolve to beat the hosts on penalties in the semi-final at Wembley, then win the final at the same venue thanks to Oliver Bierhoff's history-making – if slightly fortuitous – 'golden goal' against the Czech Republic.

The players

When Berti Vogts resigned as coach in the aftermath of the 1998 World Cup, he left no obvious successor – ushering in a rare period of instability for both the German FA and the national side. His replacement, **Erich Ribbeck**, is seen by many as a stopgap measure, and Germany's faltering progress in qualifying for Euro 2000 did nothing to calm the mood of unease.

In the absence of any obvious alternative, Ribbeck will build his squad around Ottmar Hitzfeld's Bayern Munich side, with **Oliver Kahn** as first-choice 'keeper, record international appearance holder **Lothar Matthäus** at sweeper, and **Thomas Linke** and **Markus Babbel** alongside him in the Germans' favoured three-at-the-back system.

The Bayern influence looks set to pervade midfield, too, where **Jens Jeremies** and **Mehmet Scholl** offer ballwinning and playmaking respectively. Liverpool's **Didi Hamann** is also a midfield contender while another Premiership star, Middlesbrough's **Christian Ziege**, is the most accomplished of the current crop of wing-backs – traditionally one of the key components of Germany's attacking game. Expect call-ups, too, for Hertha Berlin's creative but inconsistent duo, **Dariusz Wosz** and **Sebastian Deisler**.

Upfront, Milan's **Oliver Bierhoff** is the obvious target man, but the search continues for a worthy successor to Klinsmann's mantle, with **Carsten Jancker** of Bayern, Hertha's **Michael Preetz** and Leverkusen's **Oliver Neuville** all trying to fill the great man's boots with varying degrees of conviction.

PORTUGAL

Perhaps the most frustrating of all 16 teams participating at Euro 2000, the Portuguese go into the tournament promising nothing but instinctive, one-touch football that is a joy to behold. The prospect of them scoring the odd goal or two, let alone winning a match, is rather more remote.

The draw has not been kind to Portugal, who have outplayed both England and Germany in the past couple of years, yet lost to both. And after failing to beat Romania in either of their Euro 2000 qualifiers, they would probably rather not be resuming that particular acquaintance, either.

Yet for as long as players such as Luís Figo, Rui Costa and Sérgio Conceição are given free rein to exercise their rich footballing imaginations, Portugal will always be worth watching – and in with a chance of springing a surprise.

The country's footballing authorities have already pulled off an upset of their own, after beating off the challenge of neighbouring Spain to win the right to host the next European Championship finals, in 2004. This despite Portugal's dilapidated stadia, its poor transport infrastructure, its lack of experience at staging international events and, above all, the sheer poverty of its domestic game, which suffers an annual exodus of its finest homegrown talent to the big leagues of Spain, England and Italy, and which is plagued by corruption and mismanagement. Now it's up to the national side to prove that UEFA was right in bestowing its generous gift

Treating the ball as a friend – Luís Figo

– to prove that, on footballing grounds alone, the Portuguese will indeed be worthy hosts of the continent's showpiece event.

The pedigree

Portugal entered the qualifying rounds for the first-ever European Championship in 1959/60 but, after beating East Germany over two legs, they were crushed 5–1 by Yugoslavia in Belgrade. The side was a tidy one, but had yet to be inspired by the arrival of Eusébio, the Mozambique-born forward who would go on to become a legend with his European Cup displays for Benfica and his part in Portugal's run to the semi-finals of the 1966 World Cup in England.

The great man failed to inspire his adopted country in subsequent European Championships, however, and after a further fallow decade in the 1970s, the Portuguese had to wait until 1984 before finally making an impact. Their campaign in France began indifferently with two draws, but veteran striker Tamanini Nené's winner in the last group game against Romania, coupled with West Germany's simultaneous defeat by Spain, was enough to propel them into the semi-finals. There they would play their part in what some argue remains the greatest game in the history of the tournament, coming back from a goal down to lead the hosts 2–1 in Marseilles with a brace of goals from Rui Jordão, before ultimately losing to the genius of Platini, Tigana *et al* in extra time.

While the younger generation in that side, typified by the audacious skill of players like Diamantino and Paulo Futre, failed to fulfil its potential, its memory was kept alive by the new-look team coach António Oliveira brought to England for Euro '96. After playing the then reigning champions Denmark off the park (but only drawing 1–1) and edging past Turkey 1–0, the Portuguese took advantage of a weakened Croatia side to win their last game 3–0 and, with it, their first-stage group. That gave them a quarter-final berth against the Czech Republic – a tie between two sides whose love of improvisation should have produced a classic match. Yet once Karel Poborsky's freaky chip had put the Czechs ahead, Portugal seemed dumbstruck; they didn't so much bow out of the competition, as creep out of it, as if embarrassed that their beautiful football had produced so little in the way of attacking punch.

The players

Oliveira's successor as Portugal coach, **Humberto Coelho**, was an international defender who won 64 caps for his country during the lacklustre '70s. As such, he has placed a tad more emphasis on solidity than his predecessor, and it was no surprise that the Portuguese qualified for Euro 2000 as the second-placed team with the best record, despite taking only one point from their two meetings with Romania.

In terms of personnel, however, it's business as usual. The core of the squad remains Portugal's 'golden generation' – the players who won back-to-back World Under-20 Championships in 1989 and on home soil in 1991. Goalkeeper **Vítor Baía** is likely to captain the side, having recovered his form following a loan move back from Barcelona to his beloved FC Porto. Two more Porto players, **Carlos Secretário** and **Jorge Costa**, will play key defensive roles, alongside the formiable **Fernando Couto** of Lazio and the underrated **Dimas**, once of Juventus but now enjoying a fresh lease of life in Belgium with Standard Liège.

In midfield, the three Italian-based stars – Lazio's **Sérgio Conceição**, Fiorentina's **Rui Costa** and Parma's **Paulo Sousa** – seem certain to start if fit, as is Barcelona's matchless **Luís Figo**, ostensibly a winger but a man capable of providing a telling influence from almost anywhere. There are younger talents to provide backup, however, notably **Dani** of Ajax (and once of West Ham) and Sporting Lisbon's in-form **José Vidigal**.

Benfica strikers **João Pinto** and **Nuno Gomes**, together with Real Sociedad's **Ricardo Sá Pinto**, have decent scoring records but, with so much creativity behind them, will be under the usual pressure to perform.

ROMANIA

When Gheorghe Hagi came out of international retirement to help his country beat Hungary for the first time in their history, a Bucharest baker named a new cake after him. He was also given a racehorse and, almost as an afterthought, named Romania's Footballer of the Century. That 2–0 win over the Magyars in June 1999 had more than merely symbolic significance – it took the Romanians to the top of their Euro 2000 qualifying group, where they would remain, unbeaten, for the rest of the campaign.

Yet while Hagi has since been persuaded to postpone his retirement yet again so that he can lead his country in the Low Countries, Romania's dependence on the ageing playmaker with the size 5 boots is giving the country's football hierarchy cause for concern. Already, his influence and that of other senior players has led indirectly to the dismissal of the coach who led the Romanians through qualifying, Victor Piţurca, and his replacement, Emerich Ienei, is no more than another temporary throwback to an earlier, more glorious era.

Ienei concedes that Romania's national side will have to undergo some dramatic rebuilding after Euro 2000, but the old guard's reluctance to give new talent its chance – or the public's insistence on their continued selection – may mean that any reconstruction is a long and painful process.

Fans may expect Hagi and his fellow sorcerers to produce the odd flurry of magic during these finals, but unless Ienei can find an unlikely blend between youth and experience, his own prediction of a Romanian triumph in Rotterdam on 2 July will remain the stuff of Balkan fantasy.

The pedigree

One of only four European countries to turn up for the first-ever World Cup in 1930, Romania were similarly enthusiastic about the competition's European equivalent when it was instigated at the end of the '50s. Yet the team would make little impression at this level for decades, their poor form typified by a three-game quarter-final marathon against the old enemy Hungary in 1972, ultimately lost in neutral Belgrade after stalemates home and away. It wasn't until the mid-1980s, as Steaua Bucharest rose to the summit of European club competition under Emerich Ienei, that the Romanians made an impact on the international game.

Reaching the European Championship finals for the first time in 1984, Romania offered only the odd glimpse of skill as a talented squad suffocated under the weight of overly defensive tactics. They managed a 1–1 draw with Spain in Saint-Étienne before losing to both West Germany and Portugal, and catching the first plane home.

It was Ienei who led Romania to the 1990 World Cup finals in Italy, the core of the squad made up of Steaua players like Hagi, striker Marius Lăcătuş and sweeper Miodrag Belodedici. They reached the second round and made many friends among neutral supporters with their maverick attitude to football – a

Final wave – Dan Petrescu nears the end

breath of fresh air in an otherwise dull advertisement for the modern game.

The charm offensive continued under another former Steaua coach, Anghel Iordănescu, in America four years later, where Hagi's magic, combined with the assured defensive play of Gica Popescu and Dan Petrescu, and the impudent goalscoring of Florin Răducioiu and Ilie Dumitrescu, took Romania to the quarter-finals.

In England for Euro '96, the first signs emerged that Hagi's generation was nearing the end of its road. Romania lost all three of their games, and Iordănescu clung on to his job only because public anger was turned on the match officials who failed to spot that Dorinel Munteanu's shot against Bulgaria had crossed the line.

Yet there was still time for another hurrah at the 1998 World Cup, for which Romania had again qualified impressively. Adrian Ilie's deft strike accounted for Colombia, while Munteanu's long, late pass to Petrescu was enough to beat England and send the team through to another second-round berth, and narrow defeat by Croatia. England had made the fatal error of allowing the Romanians too much time on the ball that night in Toulouse. The question now, two years on, is whether anyone will be as generous to a group of magicians whose need to dwell before casting their spells is, if anything, even greater than it was then.

The players

It doesn't quite all begin and end with Hagi. Coach **Emerich Ienei** took a squad of entirely home-based players to a friendly tournament in Cyprus in January to assess the potential of Romania youth, and came back with a short list that included Rapid Bucharest goalkeeper **Bogdan Lobont**, who has just signed for Ajax and looks ready to step into the shoes of the experienced but accident-prone **Bogdan Stelea** of Salamanca.

Among the young defenders itching for a call-up are **Pompiliu Stoica** of Astra Ploieşti, **Bogdan Mara** (Arges-Dacia Piteşti) and **Florentin Dumitru** (Petrolul Ploieşti), but the back-line will, as always, be dominated by old hands such as Chelsea's **Dan Petrescu** and another player with English connections, **Gica Popescu**, who like his brother-in-law Hagi has spent the past couple of seasons in Turkey with Galatasaray.

Gheorghe Hagi himself, now 35 but looking much as he did a decade ago, seems likely to return to his native country after the finals, perhaps to his hometown club Farul Constanţa. But several of his fellow midfielders are still prospering abroad, among them **Dorinel Munteanu** in Germany with VfL Wolfsburg, and the more defence-minded **Constantin Gâlca** in Spain with Espanyol.

The Romanians have endured a rapid turnover in the goalscoring department in recent seasons, but that may be no bad thing. While **Adrian Ilie** (Valéncia) and **Viorel Moldovan** (Fenerbahçe) seem certain of their places in the squad, **Ioan Ganea** (VfB Stuttgart) and **Adrian Mihalcea** (Dinamo Bucharest) will press them every inch of the way.

THE TEAMS: GROUP B

BELGIUM

Twelve months before they were due to kick the first ball of Euro 2000 in the opening game against Sweden in Brussels, the co-hosts' football was in its saddest state for a generation. The domestic game was dogged by accusations of match-rigging, impoverished clubs were being forced into mergers, European competition had become a form of self-torture and, to cap it all, the national side failed to beat Luxembourg.

Something had to be done. Having given a poor account of themselves at the 1998 World Cup, Belgium's *Diables Rouges* needed a complete makeover in advance of what was supposed to be the country's most important footballing moment in three decades. Enter Robert Waseige, a quiet, grey-looking figure who replaced Georges Leekens as national coach in the summer of 1999, and immediately set about re-inventing not just the national side, but his country's whole attitude to football.

It took just one match for Waseige's impact to be felt. Having failed to score in six matches, Belgium drew 5–5 with Holland in a Rotterdam friendly, a game as liberating for the players as it was entertaining for the fans. Big wins over Morocco and (more unexpectedly) Italy followed, and a nation that had appeared to be running scared from Euro 2000 now turned as one to embrace it. The enthusiasm spread to club football like a welcome infection.

While still lagging behind France and Germany in terms of star quality, the Belgian league became the highest-scoring major league in Europe, with an average of nearly four goals per game. Advance season-ticket sales reached a ten-year high, spurred on by the revival of two of the country's biggest clubs, Brussels-based Anderlecht and Standard of Liège.

It will take more than a change of attitude to bring glory to the Belgians this summer. Their squad will be one of the weakest in the tournament, regardless of how many young players Waseige chooses to bring through. But if Belgium go down, they will at least go down smiling. And they now know they can count on fervent home support – an asset that seemed far from guaranteed a year ago.

The pedigree

The last time the European Championship finals came to Belgium, in 1972, they comprised no more than four games: two semi-finals, a third-place play-off, and the final itself. As host nations went, it seemed an odd choice. The Belgians had never made much impact on the tournament, or on the World Cup for that matter. But they had qualified impressively, beating Italy in the quarter-finals thanks to goals from the busy little midfielder Wilfried van Moer and the elegant striker Paul van Himst in Brussels.

For their semi-final against West Germany, the Belgians moved to Antwerp, a little further from the German border but not far enough to deter thousands of visiting fans, whose constant barrage of noise was a factor – if not the decisive one – in Belgium's 2–1 defeat. The team belatedly showed more aggression in the third-place play-off against Hungary in Liège, winning 2–1 with van Himst again scoring the vital goal.

Neighbours Holland denied Belgium a place in the '76 finals with a quarter-final drubbing, but in 1980 an almost identical side produced the country's best-ever display in the competition. With Jean-Marie Pfaff inspirational in goal, van Moer still pulling midfield strings and the big but mobile Jan Ceulemans in attack, the Belgians beat Spain and drew with England and Italy to top their group and book a place in the final. There West Germany would again be their nemesis – Belgium had matched them stride for stride (and goal for goal) before conceding a winner from a late corner.

Riding for a fall – Branko Strupar

The Belgians qualified for the finals again in 1984, but never recovered from being thrashed 5–0 by France in Nantes. For the remainder of the decade, the greatest achievements for wily coach Guy Thys and his unglamorous but strangely appealing team would come in the World Cup, where fourth place was attained in 1986 and England were taken to the wire four years later. After Thys had made way for van Himst, Belgium put on another good show – including a famous victory over Holland and desperately unlucky loss to the Germans – at USA '94.

The latter half of the '90s, though, was a period of steep decline. Having failed to qualify for the European finals of 1992, the Belgians also missed out on Euro '96, and performed so ineptly at France '98 that UEFA would have been justified in questioning their choice of co-host for Euro 2000. In truth, an ageing side, beset by personality clashes and forced to play grittily defensive football against its will, was never going to set the world alight.

Now Robert Waseige has reversed the trend. How far he can back Belgium up the path to respectability remains to be seen.

The players

For decades, Belgium built its ability to compete with bigger nations on continuity. After falling out with the Leekens regime, veteran stars such as playmaker **Enzo Scifo**, who made his international debut in 1984, and striker **Luc Nilis** have indicated their willingness to return to the fold. Coach **Robert Waseige** says he has no need to look at them, however, fuelling speculation that he is ready to turn his back on tradition and give youth its head at Euro 2000.

There will still be plenty of familiar names in the squad, however. Anderlecht 'keeper **Filip de Wilde**'s revival in form could see him elevated back to first choice ahead of Harelbeke's **Geert de Vlieger** and **Ronny Gaspercic** of Extremadura. Another Anderlecht man, the vastly experienced **Lorenzo Staelens**, may be given the role of organising Belgium's defence, having been moved there from midfield by Waseige. Among his fellow stoppers will be the accomplished **Philippe Léonard** (Monaco), a player under-used by Leekens, Udinese's **Régis Genaux** and Lierse's versatile **Eric van Meir**, who can play at full-back or as a more attacking wing-back, depending on the opposition.

Midfield was the area most in need of attention when Waseige took over, and while the established **Marc Wilmots** of Schalke can expect a call-up, the other likely candidates are less tried and tested. They're likely to include Parma's **Johan Walem** in the anchorman role, and the promising, attack-minded Mouscron pair of **Stefaan Tanghe** and **Yves Vanderhaeghe**.

In stark contrast to the situation prior to France '98, there is no shortage of in-form strikers in Belgium's ranks. Sheffield Wednesday's **Gilles de Bilde**, while nominally a first choice, is under pressure from two other English-based players, **Branko Strupar** of Derby and Coventry's nippy **Cedric Roussel**. Then there's **Emile Mpenza** of Schalke and his brother **Mbo Mpenza** (Sporting Lisbon), both of whom have grown in stature since leaving Belgian club football at the end of 1999, not to mention the man who moved in the opposite direction to Emile, **Michael Goossens** (Standard), and Westerlo's impressive **Toni Brogno**.

ITALY

The European Championship has never been the Italians' favourite competition, and as the latest incarnation of the tournament approaches, the omens again look far from promising. The *Azzurri* will travel to the Low Countries with what looks on paper to be one of the strongest squads in the continent. But, not for the first time, it will be a group of players big on organisation and containment, and not so hot on invention.

Italy's *Serie A* remains one of the wealthiest leagues in Europe, sustained as much by free-spending club presidents as by the passion of its local support, and shortly to be made richer still by the stock-market flotation of several major clubs. When there is no *calcio* being played, the Italian obsession for the game is fed by the continent's most educated – and most unforgiving – sporting press.

Between them, these two elements form the pincer movement which has conspired against Italian success in major tournaments since the World Cup of 1982. At the biggest clubs, homegrown players are often obliged to fulfil defensive roles in the backline or midfield, while playmaking and goalscoring duties are performed by expensive foreigners. This in turn puts intense pressure on the national coach to come up with a formula that will allow Italy to play to their strengths, yet still put on a good show.

Arrigo Sacchi was widely blamed for performing too much tactical surgery on the attractive side which promised so much but ultimately fell at the first hurdle at Euro '96. His successor Cesare Maldini, meanwhile, took the rap for Italy's overly cautious approach at the 1998 World Cup, which resulted in the now customary elimination on a penalty shoot-out.

The present incumbent, legendary 'keeper (and 1982 World Cup-winning captain) Dino Zoff, is damned if he does and

Rare attacking talent – Francesco Totti

damned if he doesn't. Italian fans fret that he is no less conservative than Maldini. But when the team's sense of adventure caused them to throw away a 2–0 lead and lose 3–2 at home to Denmark in the qualifiers, Zoff was pilloried in print...

The pedigree

With the World Cup looming so large in the Italian footballing psyche, the European Championship – whether by accident or design – has often caught the *Azzurri* in a state of transition. Yet the team's sole historical success in the competition signalled the revival of the Italian game in the modern era.

Following Italy's disastrous showing at the 1966 World Cup, a ban was imposed on foreign players in the *Serie A*. Homegrown youngsters sprang to unaccustomed prominence and, as a result, the national side was able to re-invent itself. Having beaten Romania and Bulgaria among others in qualifying, the Italians were chosen as hosts for the semi-finals and final. Valcareggi was heavily influenced by the defensive strategies of the successful Inter coach of the day, Helenio Herrera, and Italy's goalless semi-final draw with the Soviet Union in Naples is considered by some as the dullest game ever played in the European finals. It was decided on the toss of a coin, which Italy won to set up a final against Yugoslavia in Rome. Here again, the *Azzurri* had luck on their side. Outplayed by their guests and a goal down, the Italians scored from a free-kick while the referee was still moving back the defensive wall; it was allowed to stand, and after the game had finished 1–1, a replay was arranged for two days later. While Italy called up five new players, the Yugoslavs fielded an unchanged side and were well-beaten, 2–0.

The Italians have never enjoyed such good fortune in the European Championship since, though they have played some much better football. When hosting the finals for the second time in 1980, Italy were denied a place in the final despite going unbeaten through their three group games. They even lost the third-place play-off on a penalty shoot-out, to Czechoslovakia.

After the party of the 1982 World Cup, a desperate lack of firepower saw Italy failing to qualify for the 1984 European Championship at all. Four years later, in West Germany, Azeglio Vicini's young side (with Roberto Mancini and Gianluca Vialli in its ranks) won high praise for its flair but bowed out in the semi-finals to the Soviets.

There was another failure to qualify in 1992, when Arrigo Sacchi became the latest *Azzurri* coach to plead with his public for patience during rebuilding – and got it. The punters were less forgiving, however, after Euro '96, when Sacchi's insistence on chopping and changing saw Italy fall from a famous win over the Russians to defeat by the Czech Republic and a stalemate with Germany – and early elimination.

The players

A survivor of both the victorious 1968 side and the luckless 1980 model, Italy coach **Dino Zoff** knows what's needed to take his country back to the top of the European tree. Whether he has all the essential ingredients is a matter for debate. There are no problems in Zoff's old position between the sticks, where Parma's spectacular **Gianluigi Buffon** and the reliable **Francesco Toldo** of Fiorentina lead a long line of world-class 'keepers jostling for consideration. The defence looks similarly strong, particularly since the emergence of the centre-back pairing of **Fabio Cannavaro** (Parma) and **Alessandro Nesta** (Lazio) – one of the few good things to come out of Italy's 1998 World Cup campaign. If Zoff's defensive instincts get the better of him, he will add **Ciro Ferrara** of Juventus as a third stopper. The evergreen **Paolo Maldini** (AC Milan) looks set to begin his last major international tournament at left-back, while the right-sided defensive role may well be filled by a reborn **Christian Panucci** (Inter).

Italy's problems begin in midfield, where **Antonio Conte** is the obvious anchorman but where real creativity is thin on the ground. Conte's Juventus team-mates **Gianluca Pessotto** and **Alessio Tacchinardi** are both well-liked by Zoff, but he may yet surprise the nation by picking one or both of the exciting Udinese pair of **Thomas Locatelli** and **Stefano Fiore**. Another alternative would be to field Roma striker **Francesco Totti** in a more withdrawn role, similar to that occupied by Roberto Baggio during much of the 1990s.

Assuming he is fit, there should be a place for Juve's **Alessandro del Piero**, either 'in the hole' between midfield and attack, or wide on the left. The first-choice strikers will be **Christian Vieri** of Inter and Juve's **Pippo Inzaghi** – close friends who have not yet proved they can work together as a successful partnership. If the pairing continues to misfire, Italy may look to Totti or his in-form Roma team-mate, **Vincenzo Montella**.

SWEDEN

The Swedes go into Euro 2000 burdened by a curious paradox. The quiet professionalism with which they qualified for the finals, winning seven out of eight games in a group that also contained England, Poland and Bulgaria, had the rest of Europe purring its approval. Back home, however, coach Tommy Söderberg's emphasis on organisation has failed to ignite the public imagination in the same way that his predecessor, Tommy Svensson, managed during the run-up to the 1994 World Cup, in which Sweden finished a magnificent third.

Svensson was never going to be an easy act to follow. Not only did he favour an exciting brand of counter-attacking football, but the men he entrusted to play it, like forwards Martin Dahlin and Tomas Brolin, offered glimpses of real flair – a commodity not often credited to Swedish football, despite its reputation as the most creative in Scandinavia.

Yet the fall of Svensson's side was as dramatic as its rise. The likes of Dahlin and Brolin aged quickly, and when talismanic goalkeeper Thomas Ravelli hung up his gloves, Sweden's fate was sealed. The team failed to qualify for either Euro '96 or the 1998 World Cup, and the coach reluctantly stepped aside.

Söderberg's first competitive game in charge, a hard-fought 2–1 win at home to England in September 1998, set the tone for his reign – and for Sweden's Euro 2000 qualifying campaign. The coach and his influential but often overlooked assistant, Lars Lagerbäck, now believe their side can make at least the last four in the Low Countries. To do that, however, they will need to find some more strings to their bow. As Lagerbäck himself puts it: "We create chances, but we don't take them. It's something we have to work on."

The pedigree

Sweden's two greatest international football moments have come not in the European Championship, but in the World Cup – first in 1958, when they hosted the event and were beaten by Pelé's Brazil in the final, then in 1994, when Brazil again barred their way, this time in the semis.

When the Swedes got the chance to host the European finals, in 1992, they at first looked capable of sweeping all before them. A cagey opening draw with France was followed by wins over Denmark and England, with Brolin, Dahlin and target man Kennet Andersson being brilliantly supplied by Anders Limpar and Jonas Thern in midfield. In the semi-finals, Sweden were due to meet Germany in Stockholm – the same city in which the hosts had beaten the West Germans in the semis of the '58 World Cup. Yet there was to be no repeat of that achievement. The Swedes' midfield lynchpin, Stefan Schwarz, was suspended after picking up two yellow

Filling Ravelli's shoes – Magnus Hedman is an eccentrically capable 'keeper

cards in the group games, and in his absence the German playmakers Hässler and Effenberg ran riot. The final score of 3–2 to the visitors flattered Sweden.

Prior to that, the closest the Swedes had come to a place in the European finals was back in 1963/64, when qualifying-round wins over Norway and Yugoslavia earned them a quarter-final against the Soviet Union. The tie was lost 4–2 on aggregate, despite a goal in each leg from scoring legend Kurt Hamrin.

The players

With Sweden's domestic game still falling awkwardly between a modern business and an old-fashioned amateur competition, most of the players called up by coach **Tommy Söderberg** for Euro 2000 will have just finished a season playing their club football abroad. This may mean the squad boasts a higher skill level and greater tactical awareness than applied in 1992 but, arguably, could cause a problem with fitness – one of the Swedes' great assets eight years ago, when home-based players were only two or three months into their domestic summer season.

As with Denmark and Norway, there's a strong British influence on Sweden's men most likely. Coventry goalkeeper **Magnus Hedman** has become Thomas Ravelli's natural successor – not quite as eccentric, perhaps, but an equally capable shot-stopper, if prone to the odd lapse of concentration.

Elsewhere, competition for places is intense. First-choice stoppers **Patrik Andersson** (Bayern Munich) and **Joachim Björklund** (Valéncia) still rate high in Svensson's esteem, but neither has been a first-choice starter for his club during the 1999/2000 season. The veteran **Roland Nilsson**, now back in Swedish football with Helsingborgs, is still in the running for a place, as are another former star of the English Premiership, **Pontus Kåmark**, and his AIK Solna team-mate **Teddy Lucic**.

Sunderland's **Stefan Schwarz** remains a key figure as the anchor in midfield, with Sheffield Wednesday's **Niclas Alexandersson** also in the frame. Assuming Anderlecht's **Pår Zetterberg** does not reverse his decision to retire from international football, creative duties may fall at the feet of Bari's impressive youngster **Daniel Andersson**. The attack-minded **Magnus Arvidsson**, in excellent form in the German *Bundesliga* with Hansa Rostock, provides another alternative.

Along with Arvidsson, the Swedes boast many players capable of filling either midfield or forward positions with ease. Among them are old-fashioned target man **Kennet Andersson** (Lazio), Celtic's **Johan Mjällby**, **Fredrik Ljungberg** of Arsenal and Bröndby's **Magnus Svensson**. All decisions in this area of the pitch are likely to be on hold, however, while the nation waits to see if Mjällby's Celtic team-mate **Henrik Larsson**, Sweden's only truly consistent goalscorer of recent years, can recover from the double leg fracture he sustained in the autumn of 1999…

TURKEY

No team qualified for the Euro 2000 on such a tide of emotion as the Turks. With their country devastated by earthquakes and their government striving for recognition within the mainstream of European politics, Turkey's national team were playing for far more than a big payday when they took on Ireland in a two-leg play-off at the end of 1999. It showed, too. After a fortunate penalty had given them a 1–1 draw in the first leg in Dublin, the Turks dominated the return in Bursa but spurned chance after chance, forcing their fiercely devoted supporters (and tens of millions watching on television) to live on their nerve ends. Eventually the game finished goalless, and Turkey were through on the away goal.

It was a slender margin, but the Turks would argue they'd already proved they were good enough to go to the finals, having beaten Germany 1–0 in the same Bursa arena in October 1998, and held the same opponents to a goalless draw in Berlin. Then again, the side's inconsistency was underlined by a home defeat at the hands of Finland, and an inability to win in Moldova which ultimately gifted top spot in the qualifying group to the Germans.

With the core of the squad that played at Euro '96 still together and maturing by the month, the Turks hope that such crises of confidence can be avoided in the Low Countries. If they can, then a land of 65million people will celebrate as never before. If not, there will be more recriminations, more public outpourings of grief and, no doubt, the odd suicide in the apartment blocks of Istanbul and Ankara, where football really is a matter of life and death…

The pedigree

Prior to Euro '96, the Turks had never come close to reaching the finals of European football's showpiece tournament. In fact, the only major international event they'd attended was the 1954 World Cup, at which West Germany thrashed them twice, 4–1 and 7–2.

The world has moved on since then, of course, and Turkish football is no exception. Big clubs such as Galatasaray and Fenerbahçe long ago proved they were no pushovers at European level, yet the national team remained a soft touch until the appointment of Fatih Terim as coach.

Unlike the foreign coaches who'd preceded him, Terim, as Turkey's most-capped international, was able to get under the skin of his players and command their respect. They repaid him with an epic run to the 1996 European Championship finals that included wins over Sweden, Switzerland and Hungary; an estimated 20million people took to the streets to celebrate the Turks' qualification.

Once in England, the feverish support – largely from ethnic Turks living in Britain or Western Europe – continued but the team's effervescent form did not. A gritty performance against Croatia in their opening game should have been rewarded with a point, but Turkey conceded a late breakaway goal and never really recovered. Bigger losses to Portugal and Denmark followed, and Terim departed for the coach's job at Galatasaray.

The players

There's no denying that Turkey's first-choice 11 have come on in leaps and bounds since Euro '96. What may worry coach **Mustafa Denizli** is his squad's lack of strength in-depth.

Standing by – Galatasaray's Arif Erdem

Goalkeeper **Rüstu Reçber** (Fenerbahçe) is a case in point – approaching his 50th cap, he has been suffering from niggling injuries during the year, and the man most likely to deputise, **Fevzi Tuncay** (Beşiktaş), lacks first-team experience. Other key defenders, such as skipper **Ogün Temizkanoglu** (Trabzonspor) and cultured stopper Alpay Özalan (Beşiktaş), will be equally hard to replace if injuries or suspensions pile up. Both Ogün and Alpay have the ability to play the ball out of defence and instigate counter-attacks, lessening the playmaking burden that rests on **Abdullah Ercan** (Trabzonspor) and **Ümit Davala** (Galatasaray).

Upfront, the 'Bull of the Bosphorus', **Hakan Sükür** (Galatasaray), remains first choice as target man, his position cemented not just by his consistent goalscoring but also by his rapport with **Sergen Yalçın** (Fenerbahçe), who plays just behind him. If the partnership misfires at Euro 2000, expect a call-up for Hakan's Gala club-mate **Arif Erdem**.

THE TEAMS: GROUP C

NORWAY

At the end of 1998, the greatest era in the history of Norwegian football appeared to be coming to an abrupt and unforeseen end. The national side, previously unbeaten in Oslo for seven years, had lost 3–1 at home to Latvia and needed two late goals to force a 2–2 draw with Albania in the same city. Between them, those two results cast a lengthy shadow over Norway's Euro 2000 qualifying campaign and turned the normally cele-bratory home crowd – one of the team's great assets – into an openly hostile one.

It was a baptism of fire for Nils Johan Semb, the man who took over from the retiring Egil 'Drillo' Olsen as national coach after the 1998 World Cup. Olsen, whose six-year stint in the job had seen Norway's status ele-vated from European punchbags to a place in FIFA's top ten world rankings, had given plenty of notice of his desire to quit. Semb, in turn, had plenty of time to prepare for the job. Yet at first it seemed as though Olsen's charismatic presence would be sorely missed – by players, fans and domestic media alike.

Happily, Norway's qualifying section was one of the weakest, and after winning 2–0 away to Greece in March 1999, Semb's side embarked on a run of six successive victories – enough to secure top spot in the group, and win over all the critics who feared that a Viking invasion without 'Drillo' would be no force at all.

The pedigree

It's a measure of just how far Norwegian football has come in the last decade that it seems hard to imagine Euro 2000 could be the first time the national side has ever qualified for the European Championship finals. Yet the first time it most assuredly is – a fact that has already earned coach Semb a place in the country's sporting record books, regardless of how well the side performs in the Low Countries.

Norway's failure to qualify for Euro '96 was the low point of Egil Olsen's time in charge. Needing just two points from their last three games to be sure of their ticket to England, Olsen's side conceded a late equaliser at home to the Czech Republic, then lost away to both the Czechs and the Dutch – results that put the former top of the group, while the latter finished second and qualified for the finals after a play-off win over Ireland.

It was a bitter blow, but Olsen's refusal to become downcast rubbed off on his players, and the same resilience in the face of adversity paid rich dividends at France '98 when Norway, needing to beat Brazil in their final group game to stay in the competition, somehow conjured two goals in the last five minutes to win 2–1 – the greatest result in the country's footballing history.

Not that everyone was (or is) a fan of Olsen's carefully planned, percentage game. In France, the Norwegians were played off the park by a much more entertaining Morocco in their opening game, while Cesare Maldini, whose Italy team eliminated Norway from the second round with a dour 1–0 win, called them the most defensive side he had ever seen.

The criticism is water off a duck's back to the Norwegians, however. And, when you consider that the country's hapless and largely amateur representatives had managed just four wins in 44 European qualifiers before the start of the 1990s, you begin to understand why.

The players

As well as Egil Olsen's revolutionary approach to coaching, the English Premiership can claim a major role in elevating the standard of Norway's national team. It's likely that up to three-quarters of the final squad of 22 chosen by coach **Nils Johan Semb** will be called up from English clubs, or will have spent some time in England during the '90s. This despite the fact that several key members of the squad have not been first-team regulars for their Premiership clubs in 1999/2000 – Semb will be all too aware that it was the archetypal super-sub, Manchester United's **Ole Gunnar Solskjær**, whose brace of goals got Norway's qualifying campaign back on track in Greece.

One exception to the rule, however, might be in goal, where Sevilla's **Frode Olsen** may well be preferred to **Thomas Myhre** of Everton and **Espen Bårdsen** of Spurs, for his regular first-team exposure as much as anything else. **Frode Grodås**, once of both Spurs and Chelsea but now with German club Schalke, is another option.

There'll be no shortage of English influence in the back four, where Manchester United's **Henning Berg** (who often captains the side) and **Ronny Johnsen**, **Vegard Heggem** of Liverpool and Wimbledon's **Trond Andersen** can all be confident of a call-up, fitness permitting. Neither has Semb ruled out a recall for two more players with extensive Premiership experience behind them – Leeds' **Alf Inge Håland** and Bradford City's **Gunnar Halle**.

Meanwhile Rosenborg, the Trondheim side which dominates Norwegian club football, can expect to have a few representatives in the squad, not least the cultured full-back **André Bergdølmo**,

Pumping it forward – Alf Inge Håland

his more workmanlike but no less effective colleague **Erik Hoftun**, and stopper **Bjørn Otto Bragstad**.

As all too often in the past, the Norwegians lack a really gifted midfield playmaker. Most of those available for call-up are pacy and energetic, but not especially visionary. Among the favourites are Tottenham's **Øyvind Leonhardsen**, who always delivers for his country regardless of club form, **Vidar Riseth** of Celtic, and two long-serving campaigners – **Kjetil Rekdal** (Hertha Berlin), **Erik Mykland** (Panathinaikos). More radical alternatives include Leeds' **Eirik Bakke**, who got his first call-up earlier this year, and Monaco's emerging **John Arne Riise**.

Upfront, Semb favours the little-and-large combination of **Solskjær** and Chelsea's **Tore André Flo**, with **Steffen Iversen** of Spurs, the ever-reliable **Ståle Solbakken** (Ålborg) and young giant **John Carew** (Rosenborg) as alternative recipients of Norway's trademark long ball.

SLOVENIA

There are no prizes for guessing the unlikeliest of the 16 contenders at Euro 2000, or the team on whom you would get the longest odds against winning it – 80–1 on the eve of the draw for the finals in December 1999. But Slovenia don't care that they are the rank outsiders, or that there have been dark mutterings from some quarters that they don't deserve to be in the Low Countries at all.

For like the Norwegians in the 1990s and the Irish in the '80s, the Slovene team are on a mission to drag their country's attention away from more traditional sporting pursuits (in their case, winter sports, basketball and volleyball) and toward the cause of the beautiful game. It has not been easy. Slovenia, a former Yugoslav republic with a population of less than 2million, never made much of a contribution to the footballing life of the federation. Only Olimpija Ljubljana, from the capital, were regular members of Yugoslavia's old premier division, and of the 22 men called up for the last united Yugoslav squad at Italia '90, only midfielder Srecko Katanec was a Slovene.

Today Olimpija stumble from one financial crisis to another, as their gates – like many in Slovenia's top division – often fail to break into four figures. Katanec, in contrast, has become the focus for the great football crusade. A former UEFA Cup finalist with VfB Stuttgart and *Serie A* championship winner with Sampdoria, Katanec became national-team coach of Slovenia in July 1998. Despite an almost total lack of

Fairytale – Milenko Aćimović celebrates

dugout experience, his status as the most famous Slovene footballer of the modern era earned him the instant respect of his playing staff, while his emphasis on positive, attacking football brought a welcome break from customary caution.

Katanec is being similarly positive in his approach to the finals, pointing out that, as in the qualifying rounds, the draw has been reasonably kind to his team. The fact that the rest of Europe is so dismissive of Slovenia's chances will probably be an asset, too.

The pedigree

Put simply – there isn't much of it. After the country declared its independence from Yugoslavia in 1991, Slovenia was admitted as a member of UEFA and FIFA the following year, but did not begin playing competitive international football until 1994. Pitched into a Euro '96 qualifying section that included next-door neighbours Italy and Croatia, the Slovenes acquitted themselves reasonably well – they might even have beaten the Italians at home in their first game, but officials failed to spot that a Slovenian shot had crossed the line, and the game finished 1–1.

Three wins from ten games eventually condemned Slovenia to fifth place in a group of six, and the team was similarly unsuccessful in attempting to qualify for the 1998 World Cup.

Euro 2000 was a different matter. With Katanec installed as coach and their group's two strongest nations – Norway and Greece – both in transition, Slovenia began confidently. They deservedly drew 2–2 away to the Greeks, and were unlucky to lose 2–1 at home to the Norwegians. They then went six games unbeaten before losing to the same two opponents – by which time second place in the group had already been assured.

Then the fairytale really began. Drawn against the much-fancied Ukraine in the play-offs, Slovenia won their home leg 2–1 thanks to a late, Nayim-esque lob from the halfway line by Milenko Aćimović. They then travelled to Kiev, where they refused to wilt even after going a goal down to a disputed second-half penalty. When Miran Pavlin's low shot bobbled over the snow and into the Ukrainian net, history was made.

The squad returned to a heroes' welcome and, as thousands lined the streets, Aćimović spoke for a nation when he said: "I never thought I'd see so many Slovenes turn out to greet a football team."

The players

While Slovenia is not exactly a favourite destination for international players' agents, coach **Srecko Katanec** now finds the bulk of his squad playing their club football abroad, even if it's not always at the highest level. Others have gained useful European experience with the country's leading club Maribor Teatanic, which made history of its own in 1999 by becoming the first Slovene side to qualify for the Champions' League.

The acrobatic goalkeeping of **Marko Simeunović**, who has returned to Maribor from a spell in Turkish football with Sekerspor, played a big part in that European run, though he also has a capable deputy in the giant **Mladen Dabanović** (Lokeren), who was Slovenia's man between the sticks in the play-off against Ukraine.

Mainstays of the Slovenes' typically central European, three-at-the-back defence include **Aleksander Knavs** (Tirol Innsbruck), **Marinko Galić** (Maribor) and **Robert Englaro** (Atalanta), while **Ales Ceh** (Grazer AK), **Dzoni Novak** (Sédan-Ardennes), **Amir Karić** (Maribor) and **Miran Pavlin** (Karlsruher SC) keep the midfield motor ticking.

In attack, Katanec admits his team lacks a thoroughbred target man, though **Saso Udovic** (Young Boys Berne), **Milan Osterc** (Hércules Alicante) and **Milenko Aćimović** (Red Star Belgrade) can all make a nuisance of themselves. Happily, Slovenia's greatest contemporary talent, **Zlatko Zahović** (Olympiakos), provides the perfect back-up, linking the frontline with the middle of the park with elegance, authority and an uncanny eye for goal – he's averaged one every other game from his 40-plus caps thus far.

SPAIN

"We can't be regarded as favourites for this competition…we have no record to defend." The words of national-team coach José Antonio Camacho have a particular resonance, not just for the outside world but also for his domestic audience and, perhaps most important of all, for his own players. The story of Spain during the 1990s has been one of qualifying comfortably for the final stages of major international tournaments, then failing to deliver on the grand stage through rotten luck, a shortage of self-belief, poor judgement at crucial moments, or all three of these. The pundits agree that the Spaniards normally bring one of the stronger squads to big events like the World Cup and European Championship, yet the inability of those squads to fulfil their potential has become a cliché.

After yet another cruise through qualifying (Spain scored 42 goals in eight games en route to Euro 2000), coach Camacho sees it as his job to downplay his team's chances in the run-up to the main event. And he's probably right to do so. While his side is capable of playing devastating football, little of it is ever seen outside Spain itself. The players, too, have little experience of life outside the affluent but essentially rather insular world of the *Primera Liga*, where the interests of FC Barcelona and Real Madrid often conflict with those of the national team, and where the standard of football can vary wildly from week to week.

In the Low Countries, as ever, the *Selección* will be accompanied by a huge and noisy entourage of fans, while back home, millions more watch the action on television in thousands of bars from the Basque country in the north to Andalucía in the south. Yet they will all be watching in hope rather than expectation. After being so rudely awoken from their dreams on so many occasions in the recent past, the Spaniards have a healthy aversion to hype.

The pedigree

Strictly speaking, José Antonio Camacho is doing his country a disservice when he says it has "no record". Spain have, in fact, lifted the Henri Delaunay trophy – though it was back in 1964, when the competition was in its infancy. Forwards Amaro Amancio and Luís Suárez were the stars of a team that beat Romania, Northern Ireland and the Republic of Ireland before being nominated by UEFA as hosts of the semi-finals and final. Amancio's goal, deep into extra time, eliminated Hungary in Madrid, setting up a meeting with the Soviet Union in the final at the same venue.

Four years earlier, Spain's fascist dictator General Franco had forbidden his squad to play the Soviets, giving the latter a bye at the quarter-final stage and giving them a helping hand along the road to winning the first-ever European Championship. Now it was a different story – Franco saw scope for a rare propaganda coup, and took his place among a capacity

A veteran at 22 – Raúl González

120,000 crowd in the Chamartín (now Bernabéu) stadium for the big match. It was a dull day, and as rain swept through the arena, the pitch became increasingly boggy, preventing either side from playing its natural passing game. But the match did at least have a spectacular ending, Marcelino's diving header flying into the corner of the Soviet net six minutes from time, giving the home side a 2–1 victory.

The win broadly coincided with the start of a ban on foreigners in the Spanish *Liga*. Designed to improve the chances of the *Selección* in international tournaments, it in fact had the reverse effect. England beat Spain home and away to knock them out of the quarter-finals of the 1968 European Championship, while the class of '72 did not even make it that far. The ban was eventually lifted in 1973, yet Spain remained international also-rans for much of the decade, bowing out to West Germany in the European quarter-finals of 1976, and failing to win a match in their first-round group in 1980.

The trend looked set to continue with the country's disastrous hosting of the 1982 World Cup, yet within two years, a revived team – crucially playing without the enormous pressure of home support – crept almost unnoticed into the final of Euro '84. The Spaniards had reached the finals in bizarre fashion. Needing to beat Malta by 11 clear goals to deny the Dutch, they won 12–1 in Seville; UEFA viewed a videotape of the match but took no action. Once the team were in France, a late goal by Maceda against West Germany in the first round and a victory on penalties over Denmark in the semi-finals. For once it seemed that luck was running Spain's way, but in the final, against France in the Parc des Princes, the run of good fortune came to an end. In the 56th minute, Spain's goal-keeper and captain Luís Arconada allowed Michel Platini's harmless free-kick to bounce out of his hands and over the goal line, and the under-dogs never recovered; they eventually lost 2–0.

The emergence of Michel and 'the Vulture' Butragueño made the Spain of Euro '88 a more attractive side than that of four years earlier. Both men were on target as Denmark received their customary beating in the opening group fixture, but after that the Spaniards lost the plot, losing 1–0 to Italy and 2–0 to their West German hosts.

Worse was to follow when the Michel Platini, now as coach of France, again intervened to deny Spain a place at Euro '92 at all. And while Javier Clemente's side came to England four years later as one of the favourites, a desperate lack of firepower almost condemned them to another first-round exit before a late winner against Romania at Elland Road. Pitted against England at Wembley in the quarter-finals, the Spaniards rose to the occasion, knocking the confidence out of a home side that had come into the fixture on the back of a four-goal rout of Holland. Spain might have won it, too, had Julio Salinas' goal not been wrongly ruled out for offside. In the end the game finished goalless, and England, with Stuart Pearce's self-cleansing spot-kick to the fore, went through on penalties.

The players

Depending on which way you look at it, the Spaniards approach Euro 2000 with either a patched-up squad or the perfect blend of youth and experience. In fact, whoever he picks, coach **José Antonio Camacho** seems certain to be fielding one of the youngest squads in the tourna-ment, for even among the established backbone of Fernando Hierro, Josep Guardiola, Luís Enrique and Raúl, the average age is 28.

Following Andoni Zubizarreta's retirement, goalkeeping chores gen-erally fall to the man who was his understudy for so long, **Santiago Cañizares** (Valéncia), with Atlético Madrid's **José Francisco Molina** as the expected stand-in, and Real Zaragoza's **Juanmi Garcia** as the likely third choice.

If his knees are up to it, the defence will be marshalled by Real Madrid's **Hierro**, who has dropped back from his former stomping ground in midfield, with **Abelardo** of Barcelona as the other stopper, and **Enrique Romero** (Deportivo La Coruña) and **Sergi** (Barcelona) as first-choice full-backs. Other defensive options are served up by Newcastle's **Marcelino**, **Michel Salgado** of Real Madrid and the experienced **Rafael Alkorta** of Athletic Bilbao.

As he is for his club, Barcelona's **Guardiola** will be the man around whom the midfield action revolves, though he is likely to play relatively deep to allow his Barça colleague **Luís Enrique** and Bilbao's **Joseba Etxeberría** space to run into. **Vicente Engonga** (Mallorca), **Pedro Munitis** (Racing Santander) and a revived **Fran González** (Deportivo) may also see their fine club form translated into an international call-up.

While Etxeberría and his Bilbao team-mate, **Julen Guerrero**, can play in forward positions, Camacho, will surely start with Real Madrid's **Raúl** – Europe's third-highest scorer in 1998/99 – as his main striker, with Real Valladolid's **Victor**, Bilbao's **Ismael Urzáiz** and Santander's sensational youngster **Salva** all in contention for a supporting role.

YUGOSLAVIA

Seven long years after a team playing as 'Yugoslavia' was barred from appearing in the European Championship finals because of armed conflict, a side bearing the same name almost suffered a similar fate. As NATO bombs rained down on Belgrade, UEFA suspended all Euro 2000 qualifying games due to be played in former Yugoslav republics, as well as in rump Yugoslavia (essentially Serbia) itself. Many top Yugoslav players – some of whom were in the team whose invitation to Euro '92 was withdrawn at the last moment – had travelled home for a qualifier against Croatia, only to find that not only was the match postponed indefinitely, but that they had no obvious means of leaving the country. And although those that wanted to leave did get out eventually, the longer the war in Kosovo went on, the less likely it seemed that Yugoslavia would be able to fulfil its qualifying fixtures.

Happily, a peace (of sorts) was negotiated over the summer of 1999, Yugoslavia's games were hastily rescheduled, and after playing five games in as many weeks during September and October, the team emerged as the unlikely winners of their qualifying section. There was an element of good fortune about it – had Ireland not conceded a late equaliser in Macedonia while the Yugoslavs were drawing 2–2 in Croatia, the Irish would have won the group, while a politically awkward (and highly charged) play-off against moslem Turkey would have beckoned for the Slavs. But for the veterans who had been denied the chance to show Europe what they could do in '92, there was a curious justice in the hand fate now dealt.

What it all means for the finals themselves is a matter for debate. The Slavs have another veteran, 68-year-old Vujadin Boskov, as coach following the quiet removal of Milan Zivadinović when the Kosovo conflict was at its peak. This is Boskov's second spell in charge of Yugoslavia (his first was in the early 1970s), and after a club coaching career that has taken him the length and breadth of Europe, he can count among his former pupils Srecko Katanec and José Antonio Camacho, current coaches of group rivals Slovenia and Spain, with whom he won domestic championships with Sampdoria and Real Madrid, respectively.

While the pedigree, the passion and the personnel are all in place, however, the preparation is unlikely to be the best, and there is a suspicion that the miracle of simply taking part at Euro 2000 may be as much as an able but ageing Yugoslav team can hope for.

The pedigree

In the competition's formative years, Yugoslavia twice reached the final of the European Championship. Whether the current nation can claim those achievements as its own is a moot point, however, since in those days the Yugoslav line-up would commonly contain players from all ethnic groups in the federation, Croats, Bosnians, Macedonians and Albanians among them. Whatever their ethnic make-up, they were arguably the better side on both occasions – yet lost both ties.

The first disappointment came in the first finals of 1960. Having come back from 4–2 down to beat hosts France 5–4 in the semi-finals, Yugoslavia continued their policy of all-out attack in the final against the Soviet Union in the Parc des Princes. They were a goal up at half-time but should have been further in front; after the Soviets had equalised, Yugoslavia tired and were eventually muscled out of it, 2–1, after extra time.

It was a not dissimilar story eight years later. Benefitting from Alan Mullery's sending-off in their semi-final against World Cup holders England, Yugoslavia won 1–0 with a goal from their dazzling winger Dragan Dzajić. Italy were then played off the park in the final in Rome, only to be given a controversial late equaliser. A replay was scheduled for just 48 hours later, and while the Italians called up five fresh players, Yugoslavia fielded the same side – now bereft of both energy and ideas. The hosts won comfortably, 2–0.

The Yugoslavs were absent from the 1972 finals, having lost to the Soviets at the quarter-final stage, but four years later, after an exceptional side including the ageless Dzajić, Dušan Bajević and Brane Oblak had survived a quarter-final scare against Wales, Yugoslavia found itself nominated as the host nation for the final stages. Matches were split between Belgrade and Zagreb (today's Croatian capital), and in a tournament that would come to be regarded as a classic of 'total football', all four went to extra time. The hosts, alas, had the misfortune to lose both their games – their semi-final 4–2 to West Germany (after being two up at half-time), and the third-place play-off 3–2 to the Dutch.

If the Yugoslavs were guilty of playing too much football on home soil in 1976, they played too little in France eight years later, losing all three games and only finding their form when there was nothing to lose, in their last match against the hosts.

Absent from Euro '88 but among the unlikely heroes of the World Cup in Italy two years later, Yugoslavia set about qualifying

Last hurrah – Dragan Stojković

for the 1992 European Championship in fine style. The team was captained by the elegant playmaker Dragan Stojković and also boasted the likes of Dejan Savićević, Robert Prosinečki, Davor Šuker and Darko Pančev. As the qualifying campaign went on, however, so the various Croats, Slovenes, Bosnians and Macedonians gradually ruled themselves out. By the time Yugoslavia sealed qualification with a win over Austria, coach Ivica Osim was fielding what amounted to a Serb and Montenegrin eleven.

Even so, the side was confident of success in Sweden, and felt bitter at being excluded after UEFA decided it could not defy the logic of UN sanctions against Serbia, and voted to install group runners-up Denmark in the Yugoslavs' place…

The players

With two or three generations of players now having fled Yugoslavia for higher wages and stability elsewhere in the world, coach **Vujadin Boskov** has to cast a wide net to bring his squad together.

At France '98, goalkeeper **Ivica Kralj** was the only squad member to be playing club football at home. Now he's moved from Partizan Belgrade to PSV Eindhoven, and become a more complete player – though he's still not the most commanding 'keeper in Europe.

In defence, the key figure remains Lazio libero **Sinisa Mihajlović**, a player as useful for his passing ability and long-range free-kicks as his mastery of a backline. Alongside him are stoppers **Miroslav Djukić** (Valéncia) and **Nisa Saveljić** (Bordeaux), with Sampdoria's **Nenad Sakić** and Celta Vigo's **Goran Djorović** likely to fill the wing-back roles.

The veteran **Dragan Stojković** (Nagoya Grampus Eight) who played for Yugoslavia at Euro '84, continues to captain his country from midfield and remains a talismanic presence, though his trademark change of pace has gone for good. Lazio's **Dejan Stanković** offers more youthful energy, probably from one or other of the flanks, while Inter's **Vladimir Jugović** provides the anchor. In attack, Boskov must choose between the out-of-favour **Predrag Mijatović** (Fiorentina) and **Darko Kovačević** (Juventus) on the one hand, and the in-form but less flexible **Savo Milosević** (Real Zaragoza). Another veteran, **Dejan Savićević** (Rapid Vienna), offers a wildcard option, but probably not for a full 90 minutes.

THE TEAMS: GROUP D

CZECH REPUBLIC

Life has turned full circle for the Czechs since they trooped off the field at Wembley after losing the final of Euro '96 to Oliver Bierhoff's 'golden goal' for Germany. That team, which began the tournament as little-known as they were little-fancied, ended it as the heroes not just of their own country but of the whole continent, which had been seduced by the under-dogs' compact, confident football and taste for the unexpected. Those members of the squad who weren't already playing abroad quickly arranged transfers to Europe's bigger leagues, and the future of Czech football seemed brighter than at any time since the 'Velvet Divorce' split former Czechoslovakia into two countries in 1993.

The party was soon brought to a messy conclusion, however. The Czechs were grouped into the toughest of all Europe's qualifying sections for the 1998 World Cup, and through a combination of poor luck and their inabil-ity to turn possession into goals, the side failed even to get as far as the play-offs. Coach Dušan Uhrin lost the confidence of his players, some of whom refused to play for their country until his removal. In the end Uhrin did the decent thing and resigned, allowing Jozef Chovanec to take charge.

Chovanec, a veteran of Czechoslovakia's Italia '90 squad and former player-coach of the country's leading club, Sparta Prague, was a genera-tion younger than Uhrin and viewed by the players as 'one of the lads'. He persuaded rebels like Patrik Berger to return to the international fold with a promise that Uhrin's counter-attacking tactics would be ditched in favour of a more open game.

It was a gamble, but it paid off quicker than anyone in the country dared imagine. Within a year of Chovanec's appointment, the Czechs had become the first team (other than the co-hosts) to qualify for Euro 2000, coming from 2–0 down to beat Scotland 3–2 in Prague and seal top spot in their group. They went on to win all ten of their qualifying games – the best record in the competition, and enough to lift the Czechs into sec-ond place in FIFA's world rankings, behind Brazil but ahead of the World Cup holders, France.

Comeback kings – Patrik Berger (left) and Pavel Nedved stop the Scots

The pedigree

A statistician will gleefully report that on each occasion the Czechs have qualified for the European Championship finals, they have never finished lower than third. That fact, however, disguises the underlying reality that the national side which played as 'Czechoslovakia' had a constantly varying Czech component. In particular, the core of the team which won the competition in 1976 was not Czech at all, but Slovak.

The story begins on 5 April 1958, when Czechoslovakia travelled to Dublin to play Ireland in the first-ever European Championship qualifying game. The Irish won 2–0, but this was a two-leg tie and the Czechs comfortably won the return in Bratislava, 4–0. They went on to score a dozen more goals in eliminating Denmark and Romania, thereby booking a place in the final stages in France.

The semi-final draw pitted the Czechs against the Soviet Union and, in the suffocating heat of Marseille, Czechoslovakia out-ran their opposition for much of the game, only to run out of steam prematurely. They

lost 3–0, but the team's inventive midfield of Buberník, Masopust and
Popluhar was rewarded with a 2–0 victory over the host nation in the
third-place play-off.

There was to be no repeat four years later, after the Czechs had surprisingly gone out in the first qualifying round to East Germany, and in both
1968 and 1972, the team blew their chances of making the finals by losing their last group game. For the 1976 finals, however, Czechoslovakia
eliminated England and Portugal at the group stage, then exacted revenge
over the Soviet Union with a 4–2 aggregate quarter-final win.

As they would be in England two decades later, the Czechs were the outsiders at the '76 finals in Yugoslavia. Yet they beat nine-man Holland
3–1 after extra time in the semis, then shrugged off the psychological
blow of giving up a two-goal lead to West Germany in the final, winning
the game on penalties with Antonin Panenka's immortal chipped kick.

The side made a decent fist of defending its trophy in Italy four years
later, but were effectively out of the running after losing 1–0 to the Germans in their opening game, and had to be content with a third-place
play-off victory over the hosts, again achieved on penalties after a poor
game had finished 1–1.

And so to Euro '96, when the newly independent Czechs this time
managed to recover from an opening defeat by Germany, beating Italy
2–1 and drawing 3–3 with Russia to seal a quarter-final berth. Karel
Poborsky's impudent lob then accounted for Portugal, and after France were
beaten on penalties after a goalless semi-final, the tournament's forgotten
team were just one game away from glory. Patrik Berger's penalty put
them ahead in the final at Wembley, but Bierhoff's double – the second in
extra time – proved an obstacle too far.

The players

Though altered in some respects by retirements and the emergence of a
small amount of new talent, the Czech squad for Euro 2000 is likely to bear
a striking resemblance to that of Euro '96. Coach **Jozef Chovanec** spent
the early part of the year in Hong Kong with a Czech League representa-
tive selection, but few of that side are likely to make the grade just yet.

Sheffield Wednesday goalkeeper **Pavel Srníček**, an unused squad
member four years ago, is now first choice, with **Ladislav Maier** of Rapid

Vienna a capable if inexperienced deputy. Fiorentina's **Tomás Repka**, who missed Euro '96 through suspension, will marshall a backline trio also likely to feature **Petr Gabriel** (Sparta Prague) and **Karel Rada** (Slavia Prague), with **Ján Suchopárek** (Tennis Borussia Berlin) and **Radek Latal** (Schalke) as wing-backs.

The midfield is again likely to be the Czechs' strongest suit, with Atlético Madrid's **Radek Bejbl**, Lazio's **Pavel Nedved** and the Liverpool duo of **Patrik Berger** and **Vladimir Smicer** all survivors from the Euro '96 side – though some are in better club form than others. **Karel Poborsky** (Benfica) can be expected to add width, while Sparta Prague's teenage playmaker **Tomás Rosicky** and Slavia's **Pavel Horváth** offer young blood if the established formula fails.

Despite their scoring spree in qualifying, the suspicion remains that the Czechs may again find goals hard to come by at the highest level. The man in form is Anderlecht's towering **Ján Koller**, but the team has a habit of not playing to his strengths, which are almost exclusively aerial. The more versatile **Pavel Kuka** (VfB Stuttgart) has had a couple of poor seasons at club level, while **René Wagner** (Rapid Vienna) is untested. If the goals don't flow, expect Poborsky or Smicer to be pushed into more advanced positions.

DENMARK

"Like a fairytale" is how goalkeeper Peter Schmeichel describes the way his country qualified for Euro 2000. It's an analogy that's been used before in connection with Danish football, not least when the national side was summoned as a last-minute replacement for Yugoslavia at Euro '92, and ended up winning the tournament. Yet in many ways, Denmark's presence at Euro 2000 is just as unlikely, not to mention better deserved.

To many outside observers, the Danes gave a surprisingly good account of themselves at the 1998 World Cup, hammering a much-touted Nigeria in the second round and giving favourites Brazil the fright of their lives in the quarter-finals. Yet France '98 was always going to be a swansong for Denmark's most experienced outfield player, Michael Laudrup, and before

A lean machine – striker Ebbe Sand

long his younger brother Brian had also ruled himself out of international participation. With Schmeichel himself nearing the end of his career and a string of injuries to other first-choice players, coach Bo Johansson was obliged to coax a makeshift and unpromising-looking side through the Euro 2000 qualifiers.

There were some poor results, notably a goalless draw in Belarus and a home defeat by Wales in Denmark's first two games. Yet by the time the Danes had come from two down in Italy to complete their campaign with a 3-2 win, they'd won four games in a row – enough to clinch second place above Switzerland thanks to a superior record. Hapless Israel were then demolished 8–0 on aggregate in the play-offs, and the Danes had written another minor epic in their collection of fairytales.

The question now is whether there are any more chapters to be written in the 'Group of Death' at Euro 2000, or whether reality will finally dawn on Denmark after all.

The pedigree

As in other Scandinavian countries, football in Denmark was a largely amateur pursuit until relatively recently. Yet the Danes have a respectable European Championship record which stretches back to a fourth place as long ago as 1964. They had striker Ole Madsen to thank for scoring all six goals in three bone-crunching quarter-final games against Luxembourg, and once at the finals in France, the Danes were outplayed by the Soviet Union in their semi-final and by Hungary after extra time in the third-place play-off.

As Denmark's idealistic approach to the game was overtaken by the modern era of international transfers and big salaries in the late 1960s and early '70s, the national side lost its competitive edge and did not make another appearance until 1984, when they qualified at England's expense. The team, a first incarnation of 'Danish Dynamite', was a potent mixture of pace and individual skill. At the finals, they quickly overcame losing their first game to hosts France by knocking eight goals past Yugoslavia and Belgium, and would have set up another encounter with the French had they not lost their semi-final to Spain on penalties.

Euro '88 saw Michael Laudrup take over the spotlight from the likes of Allan Simonsen and Preben Elkjær, yet the team was not quite the sum of its parts and lost all three of its group games in West Germany that year.

Four years on, and with Michael Laudrup now refusing to play, it was if anything a weaker side that was edged out of top spot in the qualifiers by Yugoslavia – only to be invited to the finals after the Yugoslavs were booted out. Coach Richard Møller Nielsen called together what players he could (many were already on holiday at the end of the European domestic season), and somehow Denmark edged through the tournament in Sweden, gradually gaining in fitness and cohesion as they went.

After a dour goalless draw with England and a defeat by the Swedes, a 2–1 win over a surprisingly inert France put the Danes in the semi-finals, where Holland were held 2–2 and beaten on penalties. In the final, Denmark caught Germany in sluggish mood, and once John Jensen's long-range flyer had put them ahead in the first half, their confidence became unshakeable. A second goal by Kim Vilfort, plus a series of saves from Schmeichel, made the ending as perfect as could be.

At Euro '96, however, the story turned sour. Møller Nielsen's counter-attacking tactics now held no surprises for opponents, and the likes of Portugal and Croatia made Denmark look one-dimensional in attack. The Portuguese were held 1–1, but the Croatians, with Davor Šuker rampant, won 3–0, effectively bringing Danish tenure of the Henri Delaunay trophy to an end.

The players

Denmark's Swedish-born coach **Bo Johansson,** who succeeded Møller Nielsen after Euro '96, found himself having to search far and wide for players during qualifying. Yet for all its disparate sources, his Denmark side has remarkable team spirit. Goalkeeper **Peter Schmeichel** (Sporting Lisbon) is, inevitably, a big factor in keeping everyone together. Now 36, the Danes' most-capped international is still a commanding presence both in goalkeeping terms and in relation to the rest of the team.

The defence Schmeichel shouts at has Chelsea's experienced **Jes Høgh** as its lynchpin, with **Jan Heintze** (PSV Eindhoven), **Søren Colding** (Brøndby) and **René Henriksen** (AB Copenhagen) completing Johansson's preferred flat back-four.

In midfield, the formidable bulk of **Stig Tøfting** (MSV Duisburg) holds Denmark's shape together while **Thomas Helveg** (AC Milan), **Martin Jørgensen** (Udinese) and **Allan Nielsen** (Tottenham) add the creative touches. **Jon Dahl Tomasson**, once an expensive flop at Newcastle but reborn since moving to Feyenoord, offers another option in this area but may be preferred 'in the hole' behind target man **Ebbe Sand** (Schalke). **Peter Møller** (Real Oviedo), a goalscoring hero at France '98 who has done little since, may earn a recall as a standby striker.

FRANCE

The French begin the new millennium with a big question to answer. Will their victory in the 1998 World Cup turn out to be only the start of a golden era, or merely an elegant ending to a more modest one? The evidence from France's Euro 2000 qualifying campaign is inconclusive. Roger Lemerre's side, initially showing little change in personnel from that of his predecessor Aimé Jacquet, were worryingly inconsistent, pulling off a fine win over Russia in Moscow, but losing to the same opposition in Paris, drawing in Iceland, and struggling to beat the likes of Andorra and Armenia. In the end, only Ukraine's late equaliser away to Russia allowed the French through without having to go through the lottery of the play-offs.

Having got this far, Lemerre must now impose his own personality on the squad. Jacquet's legacy of a world champion team may have looked perfect but, two years on, the defence is looking ponderous against quick-witted forward lines, the midfield lacks width, and goals – never that easy to come by, even when the French were winning the World Cup, remain harder to find than they should be for a team which is so comfortable in possession.

In the long term, France's domestic game – booming in the afterglow of World Cup glory – and admirable youth structures should ensure a healthy future for the national team. The immediate issue, though, is whether the current side can rediscover its momentum and add a European crown to the global one already in the trophy cabinet.

The pedigree

Since it was a Frenchman, Henri Delaunay, who had done most to promote the idea of a European football championship, it was fitting that the first finals should be held in France. The year was 1960, and the French public, like much of Europe, was ambivalent about the new tournament. So it was that only 26,000 fans turned up at the Parc des Princes to see France's semi-final against Yugoslavia. Those who did witnessed a classic, albeit with a surprising outcome – the French, without star players Raymond Kopa and Just Fontaine, were 4–2 up after an hour, yet allowed the Yugoslavs to come back into the game and win it, 5–4. An even smaller crowd then saw France lose the third-place game, 2–0, to Czechoslovakia.

After that, French football's long, lean spell ensured there would be no further participation in the final stages of the competition until 1984 – and even then, *les Bleus* needed the privileges of host nation to qualify automatically. France had played brilliantly at the 1982 World Cup, however, and it was broadly the same line-up, with the classic midfield trio of Michel Platini, Jean Tigana and Alain Giresse, that took the bull by the horns in the European Championship.

Things began quietly with a 1–0 win over Denmark in Paris, but then a Platini hat-trick prompted a 5–0 steamrollering of Belgium in Nantes, and the French completed their group games with a gloriously open 3–2 win over already eliminated Yugoslavia in Saint-Étienne. Another 3–2 triumph, this time over Portugal in the Marseilles semi-final, had the world's media purring its praise, and while France's 2–0 defeat of Spain in the final was more prosaic, there was no doubt they were the best team in Europe, while Platini was similarly the continent's most complete all-round footballer.

Yet while the side would make one more impressive appearance at the 1986 World Cup, France failed to make it to the finals of Euro '88, the country's old bugbear of being unable to beat East European opposition returning to haunt them in the qualifiers.

By the time Euro '92 came around, a new generation of players had evolved, playing under the auspices of Platini, the architect of the '84 victory who was now national coach. Platini's side included such attacking talents as Eric Cantona and Jean-Pierre Papin, yet bizarrely, given their instincts and those of their boss, France approached the finals in Sweden with a defensive strategy. It backfired horribly, the French went out after the group stage, and Platini quit.

Four years later, Papin and Cantona were both omitted from a more workmanlike squad brought to England by new coach Aimé Jacquet, who put the emphasis on teamwork and possession football. With the likes of Didier Deschamps and Marcel Desailly having grown up together in

France's footballing academies, it was a sensible policy. And if the team had possessed an instinctive goalscorer, it might have taken the French beyond the semi-finals – where they lost to the Czech Republic on penalties after a goalless 120 minutes.

The players

Like the Germans and, to a degree, the English, the French have a serious paring-down exercise to perform before arriving at a final 22 for Euro 2000. Echoing the strategy of his predecessor prior to the '98 World Cup, coach **Roger Lemerre** called 36 players together at the start of the year for combined full and 'A' internationals, but the exercise produced more

Pause for thought – Zinedine Zidane

questions than answers. Now it's up to the coach himself to decide how far he wants to depart from the Jacquet blueprint.

Fabien Barthez (Monaco) in goal seems certain to provide continuity from France '98, with Lemerre indicating a preference for Marseille's **Stéphane Porato** or Bordeaux's **Ulrich Ramé** as back-up, as opposed to the experienced **Bernard Lama** (Paris Saint-Germain).

In defence, the old stager **Laurent Blanc** (Inter) is sure of a place in what will be his last major finals, with **Frank Leboeuf** (Chelsea) alongside him and **Marcel Desailly** (Chelsea) dropping back from midfield to offer extra cover. Parma's **Lilian Thuram**, Roma's **Vincent Candela** and Bayern Munich's **Bixente Lizarazu** are three players fighting over two wing-back places, while home-based players such as **Jerôme Bonnissel** (Bordeaux) and **Martin Djetou** (Monaco) will also stake a claim.

The Arsenal midfield duo of **Emmanuel Petit** and **Patrick Vieira** are pretty much a given, but there is intense debate on how to relieve some of the creative burden from **Zinedine Zidane** (Juventus), hero of the '98 World Cup final. One possibility would be to play Bordeaux's lively **Sylvain Micoud** alongside, or to put more emphasis on the flanks, where **Robert Pires** (Marseille) is in excellent club form.

As ever, though, the biggest French dilemmas lie upfront. Kaiserslautern's **Youri Djorkaeff**, Monaco's **David Trezeguet** and Arsenal's **Thierry Henry** all look good for a nod, despite none of them having scored consistently for their country. **Stéphane Guivarc'h** (Auxerre) and **Nicolas Anelka** (Real Madrid) may also enter the running. But it may be that a more conventional target man, such as Bordeaux's **Sylvain Wiltord** or **Lilian Laslandes**, or Lyon's **Tony Vairelles**, will provide the answer to Lemerre's prayers.

HOLLAND

The contrast between the Dutch attitude to Euro 2000 preparation and that of their co-hosts, the Belgians, could scarcely be greater. Whereas the Belgians have been forced to re-invent themselves in order to produce anything like a competitive level of football, the Dutch have been afflicted by a curious apathy, born of having a settled side, confident in its abilities and forced – because of the hosts' automatic qualification for the tournament – to play nothing but friendlies for two years.

"You can't judge Pavarotti by what he sings in the shower" was coach Frank Rijkaard's standard retort to media critics (including the great Johan Cruyff) who accused his players of complacency and their manager of an inability to motivate them while Holland struggled through a series of 11 consecutive draws. A 2–1 win at home to Germany in February silenced those critics for a while, but Rijkaard knows that his popularity, always a fragile commodity since his surprise appointment as successor to Guus Hiddink in 1998, is only as good as the last *Oranje* display.

Yet Holland are among the pre-tournament favourites for good, solid reasons. The squad has no obvious weak spots, it is experienced without being overly so, and it will have the bonus of home support. Perhaps most significantly, Rijkaard, for all his lack of a track record in coaching (maybe even because of it), has maintained an excellent spirit among his players, avoiding the in-fighting which has bedevilled the Dutch so often in the past – and which characterises so much of the media reaction to his work.

The pedigree

Strange though it may seem for one of the past winners of the tournament, the Dutch have had only limited success in the European Championship. They refused to enter the inaugural event, and after they'd been persuaded of the tournament's worth and decided to try to qualify for the 1964 finals, they were beaten 2–1 at home by Luxembourg – still one of the most embrrassing results in Holland's footballing history.

Things got little better before the arrival of Johan Cruyff's 'total football' side in the early 1970s. Having introduced the world to the idea of fluidity and players performing in interchangeable positions at the 1974 World Cup, it seemed only natural that the Dutch should play a major part in the European Championship finals two years later. And play a part they did, albeit not as successfully as many had predicted. Having posted a famous 5–0 victory over Belgium en route to the finals, Cruyff and company found Czechoslovakia's counter-attacking game much harder to break down in their semi-final in Zagreb, and lost 3–1 after having two men sent off. A win in the third-place play-off provided its usual scant recompense.

By the time the next Championship came along, Cruyff had retired from international football and other influential figures like Johnny Rep and the van de Kerkhof brothers were reaching the end of their careers. The structure of the 1980 finals in Italy also acted against Holland's free-form approach to the game, and they failed to get beyond the first-round group stage.

Within four years the Dutch had re-invented themselves with a fitter and more structured side that included youngsters Frank Rijkaard, Ruud Gullit and Marco van Basten. They were denied a place at the 1984 finals by Spain's unlikely 12–1 win over Malta in the qualifiers, and at the 1986 World Cup by Belgium's away-goals playoff win.

Looking back – Dennis Bergkamp

But there was to be no mistake for Euro '88, despite Holland being forced to replay a qualifier against Cyprus because of crowd trouble in Rotterdam. There was trouble at the finals in West Germany, too, but happily for the Dutch, their results were not affected. Resilient as well as resourceful, the team bounced back from defeat by the Soviet Union to eliminate England on the back of a van Basten hat-trick, then edged past Ireland with a late winner from Wim Kieft.

The semi-finals saw another late winner – this one, from van Basten, owing far less to luck, and bringing with it the bonus of putting out the West Germans, Holland's most bitter foe. The final in Munich reunited the Dutch with the Soviets, who were forced to field a much weaker side than in the first round. It was a well-balanced game, but a first-half header from Gullit and a stunning volleyed second from van Basten gave Holland a deserved victory and their country its first major prize in international football.

It was a prize the Dutch made a surprisingly hamfisted defence of at Euro '92. Despite the arrival of new talents such as Dennis Bergkamp, Holland failed to capitalise on another famous triumph over the Germans in the group stage, and bowed out rather meekly to Denmark on penalties in the semi-finals.

In England four years later, the Dutch self-destructed in a hail of off-the-pitch disputes. Edgar Davids was sent home following a 4–1 mauling by the hosts at Wembley, and with the squad also hit by injuries, another meek shoot-out exit, this time at the hands of France in the quarter-finals, seemed somehow inevitable.

The players

Part of the problem facing coach **Frank Rijkaard** has been that, with his side so settled, the battle for squad places is not as fierce as it might be. **Edwin van der Sar** is established as first-choice 'keeper, his credentials having been improved by his 1999 move from Ajax to Juventus, while Liverpool's **Sander Westerveld** is the likely deputy.

For a long time it seemed van der Sar would rejoin his former Ajax coach Louis van Gaal at Barcelona and, had he done so, it would have lifted the number of Barça men likely to be named in the Dutch squad to eight. As it is, coach Rijkaard could name a back four composed entirely of Barcelona players, with **Philip Cocu** and **Ronald de Boer** as stoppers, and **Michael Reiziger** and **Winston Bogarde** the full-backs. A more likely formation would see Manchester United's **Jaap Stam** and/or Rangers' **Arthur Numan** in central defence, with de Boer joining his brother Frank in midfield.

Clarence Seedorf (Inter) and **Edgar Davids** (Juventus) offer both creativity and solidity in the middle of the park, with Barça's **Boudewijn Zenden** edging ahead of Arsenal's **Marc Overmars** as the man favoured to offer width. Overmars' club-mate **Dennis Bergkamp** is likewise not guaranteed a place in the Dutch starting line-up, with yet another Barça man, **Patrick Kluivert**, PSV's **Ruud van Nistelrooy**, **Jimmy Floyd Hasselbaink** of Atlético Madrid and **Roy Makaay** of Deportivo all in form and vying for a slice of the attacking action.

THE HOST CITIES:

AMSTERDAM

Fans visiting Amsterdam find it strangely bereft of football culture. Sure, they love its peaceful vibe, its canals, bars and coffee shops, but…where's the footie?

The answer is at a futuristic superdome on the city's south-eastern edge. The Amsterdam Arena, where classic European club Ajax play their football, was opened in August 1996 with a friendly against AC Milan. Queen Beatrix did the Mexican wave with 51,000 other spectators, all season tickets were quickly snapped up and, despite justified criticism of the turf and lack of atmosphere, plans were laid for an entertainment complex to complement Europe's newest major football venue.

It looked like Amsterdam had a ground to challenge favoured Feyenoord's in the international stakes, but Rotterdam city council outbid their cautious rivals for the right to stage the Euro 2000 final. With Ajax going off the boil, average gates dipped below 45,000, and Arnhem has since stolen a lot of the Arena's thunder with its novel Gelre Dome stadium.

Still, Amsterdam city council and the corporate investors who ploughed some £50million into the project are happy. The Arena is regularly hired out for shows, while the on-site museum, shop and guided tours (see panel) bring in daily revenue.

Yet still visitors beg the question, where's the football? The Jordaan area, where Dutch stars Ruud Gullit and Frank Rijkaard once played together in the street, has been yuppified. Amsterdam is a one-club town, with none of the tension and colour that a big inner-city rivalry can provide. That said, it is still a great city to stay, look around, have a night out in – and watch a game of football.

Getting there

Schiphol airport is well-served from many British provincial airports as well as from London. A **fast train service** (every 15mins daytime, hourly at night, journey time 20mins) connects Schipol with **Centraal station**, hub of Amsterdam's transport network and a short walk from Dam square.

Many trains go on to other cities after calling at Amsterdam Centraal – don't miss your stop.

The seven-hour **train journey** from London Waterloo International (change at Brussels Midi from Eurostar to Thalys) terminates at Centraal. **Eurolines buses** terminate at Amstel station, a 20min metro journey from Centraal.

Motorists should allow at least an hour and a half to do the 45-mile run from the **Hook of Holland** to Amsterdam along the A4/E19, perhaps twice that in Mon-Fri rush hours, when the entire stretch from The Hague to Schipol can be bumper-to-bumper.

Venue verdict – the Amsterdam Arena

To easiest way to get to the ground is to take metro line #54, direction Gein, which runs from Centraal through three zones (stamp four bars) to Bijlmer. Allow 15mins. The Arena is ahead of you as you turn left down the stairs from the platform.

The stadium is colour-coded in two tiers – yellow (upper) and pink (lower). By comparison with some Euro 2000 venues, the Arena has a relatively small number of lowest-priced category tickets, allocated in narrow sections behind each goal.

By the metro entrance you'll find three soulless, upmarket bars. Of the three, the *Klein Arena*, right out of the metro exit, is the most convivial. A better bet is *Soccer World*, by the stadium entrance, a two-floor bar/restaurant part-owned by the de Boer twins, Frank Rijkaard and Danny Blind. The TV screens and walls depict football's legends, while spirits hang from the goalnet behind the bar. A small beer counter operates by the door for the pre-match rush.

At the stalls inside the ground (where the only beer on sale is low-alcohol), you'll have to pay for things with an Arena Card, available by charging your credit card in the machines, or by exchanging for guilders at a till.

The official Ajax Fanshop is by the main entrance (Mon–Fri 9am–6pm, Sat–Sun 10am–5pm), with aftershave and clogs on sale in a designer atmosphere. Meanwhile, Johan Cruyff (in video form) welcomes visitors to Ajax's entertaining two-floor club museum (open daily 9am–6pm but *not* on events days, f12.50, ☎020/311 1333) by the main entrance. Plenty of audio-visual material and well-documented displays illustrating the club's century-old history. Tours of the stadium are also available during the same hours for f12.50, while a combined ticket with museum entry is f25. Advance booking is advised for the tour.

Getting around

Most of central Amsterdam is accessible by foot or bicycle, but buses, trams and a three-line metro network run on the **Strippenkaart system**. Most journeys you'll make will only take in one zone, so stamp two bars – the stamp is valid for one hour. Transport runs 6am–midnight, after which five hourly night bus routes take over. A day ticket (*dagkaart*, f10) also covers night buses. A two-day ticket is f15.

Taxis can be ordered from a rank, or by phoning ☎020/677 7777 – you can't hail them down. Cabs are expensive – f5.80 initial charge, then f2.85 per km, rising to f3.25 midnight–6am – and often slow in Amsterdam's crowded streets.

If you want to travel in style – and you don't mind being surrounded by tourists – hop aboard

Big and bold – the Amsterdam Arena

the **Canal Bus** (daily 10am–6pm, f22 for a day ticket), which serves Centraal station, Leidseplein and Westerkerk every 30mins.

If you want to **rent a bicycle**, *Take-A-Bike* at Centraal station charge f8 per day and require a f200 deposit, while *Bike City* at Bloemgracht 70 charge f12.50 per day, with f50 and your passport as deposit.

There are four **tourist offices** in town: one inside Centraal station (Mon–Sat 8am–7.30pm, Sun 9am–5pm); one just outside it (daily 9am–5pm); another on the corner of Leidsestraat and Leidseplein (Mon–Sat 9am–7pm, Sun 9am–5pm) and one at Stadionplein (Mon–Sat 9am–5pm).

The tourist department produces an English-language **listings guide**, *What's On In Amsterdam* (monthly, f4). The free Dutch-language monthly *Uitkrant* has more detailed nightlife information.

Staying over

If you're not too fussy about sharing with strangers, the **Flying Pig Palace**, Vossiustraat 46 (☎020/400 4187, fax 020/400 5159), is a good-value hostel near Leidseplein with kitchen facilities and no curfew – take tram #2 or #5 from Centraal. Slightly upmarket is the **Globe Hotel**, a short walk from Centraal at Oudezijds Voorburgwal 3 (☎020/421 7424, fax 020/421 7423), with a choice of two- to six-person rooms (f40–60 each) and dorms (f30 each), many with canal views; the 24-hour **Sports Café** downstairs has Sky Sports, pub grub, English breakfasts and Heineken at f7.

Amsterdam has plenty of two- or three-star hotels but they can vary enormously in quality. The **Casa 400** at James Wattstraat 75 (☎020/665 1171, fax 020/663 0379) is not that central but close to Amstel train and tram station and also handy for the Arena. It offers a choice of single, two-, three- and four-bedded rooms with the doubles starting at f255 – ask for an Arena view. There's a large bar area downstairs and a summer terrace. Smaller and closer to the centre of town in the Leidseplein area is the **AMS Trianon**, J W Brouwersstraat 3–7 (☎020/673 2073, fax 020/673 8868). This has doubles from f260, singles for f210, a good-value pizzeria downstairs and car parking available (daily charge). A Schipol airport shuttle bus stops close by, and if they don't have room they can check for space at other Amsterdam hotels in the same chain.

Eating, drinking, clubbing

Visitors to Amsterdam cluster around three main patches. The red light district (out of Centraal station, go straight up Damrak and turn left at the *Grasshopper* coffee shop), full of lads on beanos; the Rembrandtplein, neon, tacky and overpriced; and the Leidseplein. Bars fall into three categories: the designer variety; dirty old *bruine kroeg*, or brown cafés; and coffee shops, or 'smokings', which attract tourists. Nightclubbing is also concentrated in the centre – check out the flyers at *Midtown Records*, Nieuwedijk 104, to see which DJs are in town.

For food, try **Balraj**, Binnen Oranjestraat 1, an Indian restaurant off Haarlemerdijk with vegetarian options; **Bojo**, Lange Leidsedwarsstraat 51, a fine-value Indonesian in the Leidseplein area that's open until 2am, 4am Sat–Sun; **Keuken van 1870**, Spuistraat 4, a one-time soup kitchen, now a cheap, popular, centrally located eaterie serving Dutch standards;

or **Van Beeren**, Koningstraat 54, an excellent lunchtime choice in the red-light district, with large portions of *stamppot*, a traditional dish of mashed potato and cabbage which is better than it sounds.

On the bar front, **Bobby Haarms** at Utrechtstraat 6, just off Rembrandtplein, is run by ex-Ajax player Haarms and packed with souvenirs (closed Sun); **Café Hendrik VIII**, Prins Hendrinkstraat 83, is a younger Ajax fans' bar diagonally left out of Centraal, with framed posters, scarves, badges and a big screen for TV games; and **Meerzicht**, on the corner of Middenweg and Brinkstraat, is opposite where Ajax's old de Meer stadium once stood, a friendly, local football bar with a signed pic of former neighbour Johan Cruyff – take tram #9 to Brinkstraat from Centraal.

The best place in town to see a live band is **El Paradiso**, a former church at Weteringschans 6–8 (tram #1, #2, #5 or #11 from Centraal), while **Escape**, Rembrandtplein 11, is large, popular techno club with a varied selection Tue–Sun, and top foreign DJs invited to the *Chemistry Club* on Sat – admission f15–35.

ARNHEM

The most futuristic stadium hosting Euro 2000 matches is not in Amsterdam but in Arnhem, close to the Dutch border with Holland, where local club Vitesse play at the Gelre Dome – a stunning piece of contemporary sports architecture that was the personal pride and joy of club president Karel Aalbers. Legend has it that the idea came to him when opening a box of matches to light one of his famous cigars – not only a movable roof (the Amsterdam Arena has that), but a movable pitch, which could be rolled away after the match and the venue rearranged for other entertainment, that very evening if necessary.

After rescuing Vitesse from bankruptcy in 1985 and helping them win promotion to Holland's top flight four years later (they've never been relegated since), Aalbers turned his attention to the club's home. He refused to become downhearted after the city council rejected his plan to rebuild Vitesse's old Monnikenhuize ground, and enlisted the help of German architect Joseph Wund in turning his dreams into reality. After years of

A roof with a view – Arnhem's Gelre Dome

fund-raising, Aalbers finally persuaded the powers-that-be that his project was worth a £43million investment.

Since it was inaugurated in 1998, the Gelre Dome has become a drain on Vitesse, whose narrow failure to qualify for the 1999 Champions' League made it impossible for the club to maintain its schedule of debt repayments. With creditors losing patience, Aalbers resigned as president in January 2000, while the club's sponsor NUON, a local energy company, pledged a rescue package worth some £7million.

As a feat of engineering, however, the Gelre Dome still takes the breath away, while the city of Arnhem, capital of Holland's Gelderland province, is a lively if not overly attractive place – much of its centre had to be rebuilt after the devastation of World War II, and it shows.

Getting there

The quickest way to get to Arnhem from other cities within Holland or Belgium is **by train**. There are direct services from Amsterdam Centraal (direction Nijmegen, service half-hourly, journey 1hr 15mins), while passengers travelling from Rotterdam and Belgium can change on to the Arnhem line at Utrecht.

Motorists arriving at the **Hook of Holland** should take the A15/E31 east in the direction of Nijmegen, then the A325 north toward Arnhem. Coming from Amsterdam, the quickest route is the A2/E35 south as far as Utrecht, then the E35/A12 east to Arnhem.

Getting around

You'll see all you need to see of central Arnhem on foot. The main train and bus stations are next to each other on Stationsplein, a little north-west of the centre, and the VVV **tourist office** (Mon–Fri 9am–5.30pm, Sat 9am–4pm) is also here and can book accommodation for you if you've turned up on-spec.

Staying over

Arnhem has a real shortage of reasonably priced hotels, particularly in summer when the city does a brisk trade in visits from war veterans. The **Hotel Pension Parkzicht**, a 15min walk east from the station at Apel-doornsestraat 16 (☎026/442 0698), has rooms for between one and six people for as little as f50 per person per night, depending on the size of

Venue verdict – the Gelre Dome

The stadium is located on the southern fringes of Arnhem, close to the German border. Regular shuttle buses are laid on from various points in town (including the main train station) on ordinary matchdays, and these are expected to be increased in number for Euro 2000 fixtures. Alternatively, you can take municipal bus #7 or #43 as far as Batavierenweg — you'll take the stadium as you get off.

There are large car parks around the Gelre Dome and these are signposted from the A12/E35 (Amsterdam and Utrecht) and the A325 (Nijmegen) motorways.

When first opened in 1998, the Gelre Dome had capacity of 26,600. This has been increased to 30,000 for the tournament, but the basic layout of the ground remains the same, with four stands named according to their geographical location. Seat pricing for Euro 2000 is beautifully simple, with all seats in the Oost and West stands being in the high-est price category, those in the upper part of the Noord and Zuid ends medium, and those at the front behind either goal the cheapest.

All the seats have been constructed from recyclable materials, and are surprisingly comfortable. The pitch you can see from them is actually housed within its own con-crete container, which weighs 11,000 tonnes and can be rolled away on steel strips using four computer-controlled hydraulic motors. The whole process takes no more than four hours.

While you're waiting, *Charly's Bar* on the walkway that surrounds the Gelre Dome is the handiest spot for a pre-match drink.

the room. Just off the same street at Paterstraat 1 is the **Hotel Rembrandt** (☎026/442 0153), offering a narrower range of accommodation but at similar prices.

Rather more upmarket, but conveniently located opposite the station, is the **Best Western Hotel Haarhuis**, Stationsplein 1 (☎026/442 7441, fax 026/442 7449), with doubles from f240 per night (three-night minimum stay during Euro 2000), a bar, an à la carte restaurant, a fitness centre and other amenities. Motorists wishing to avoid the centre of Arnhem could try the **Mercure Postiljon Arnhem**, Europaweg 25 (☎026/357 3333, fax 026/357 3361), which offers free parking and is just off the A12 (exit 26, signposted Arnhem-Noord) and the A50 (exit 20). There are double rooms for f275 per night, substantial buffet breakfast included.

Eating, drinking, clubbing

Arnhem's nightlife centres around the Korenmarkt, a 5–10min walk southeast of the train station along Utrechtse Straat. The area is best-known for its pavement cafés, many of which serve decent food. For dedicated restaurants, try the **Pizzeria do Leone** at Korenmarkt 1 or for Mexican food, **Amigo**, at Pauwstraat 14.

Among the bars, **de Schoof**, Korenmarkt 37, is the big favourite with Vitesse Arnhem fans, while a more varied clientèle patronises **le Grande Café** at Korenmarkt 16. Dedicated anoraks should check out **Papillon**, close to Vitesse's old Monnikenhuize home at Weverstraat 34a, where fans still gather to reminisce about the good old days before professional football, retractable pitches and Spice Girls concerts…

BRUGES

Belgium's leading tourist city plays host to the country's second biggest football team, Club Bruges, and their groundshare neighbours Cercle. 'Club', as they are known to all, represent the pride of Flanders, working class and Flemish-speaking, and gain support from all over the region.

Throughout Belgium, Club are very much the neutrals' favourite, famed for their team spirit and honest endeavour. In Bruges itself, support for the

From 'Olympic' to 'Jan Breydel' – the cranes make the difference

two teams is divided 50–50, but any cross-town rivalry pales next to the mutual hatred of Anderlecht – the chance of Flanders getting one over on the fat cats from Brussels is more important than the local derby match.

Football was first played in Bruges at the English College in the district of Sint-Andries west of town, where the Jan Breydel stadium – formerly the Olympiastadion – is now sited. Both clubs were founded in the 1890s, Cercle's players being mainly upper-class Dutch and Englishmen, later local, academic Catholics. Sadly, Cercle were relegated in 1997, but Club continue to be one of the most successful teams in the country, even if their old European heyday of the late 1970s is starting to feel rather a long way off.

Bruges is a small town. Players of both sides mix socially, and the local football community is refreshingly tight-knit and friendly. Local people are friendly to visitors, too, remaining remarkably tolerant given the millions of day-trippers who are drawn to the city's beautifully preserved medieval centre every year. So long as you don't make the mistake of trying to speak French, you'll be fine.

Getting there

Bruges is a stop on the main **train line** between the Belgian coast and Brussels, about 15mins from the former and an hour from the latter. There are also direct trains to/from Liège (service hourly, journey 2hrs) and connections with most of the Dutch host cities via Brussels Midi.

Motorists arriving by ferry at **Ostend** have no more than a 20min drive to the town along the A10/E40, and Bruges is just as accessible from the

Venue verdict – the Jan Breydel

For Euro 2000, special buses will be laid on from Stationsplein, in front of Bruges train station, to the ground, a 10min ride away, for the same 40BF ticket as municipal buses. The shuttles will then wait at the end of Olympialaan until after the game. If you'd prefer to have a little more time on your side, bus #5 or #15 from the station to Sint-Andrieskerk will drop you right by the best bars on Gistelsesteenweg (see below), near the stadium.

Car parking near the ground is probably best not attempted. Instead, leave your wheels in the multi-storey buried underneath central Zand square, and catch a bus or taxi out to Sint-Andries from there — allow 15–20mins.

The Jan Breydel is Belgium's only major groundshare, and a successful one at that. Its recent conversion to a 30,000 all-seater for Euro 2000 (for which the name was changed from Olympia to Jan Breydel, a legendary Flemish war hero) involved the reconstruction of the Noord and Zuid stands behind either goal. Club and Cercle have an equal share of the facilities, and each has its own club bar and office, either side of the VIP/press entrance in the main (West) stand. Each club pays an equal share of its gate money to the local council, which built the ground in 1975.

For the purposes of Euro 2000 ticketing, almost the whole of the West and Oost stands are in the highest price category, while the bulk of the Noord and Zuid ends are classed as medium. There are small areas of lowest-priced seats in each corner of the ground, and at the front of the Noord and Zuid stands.

For a swift half, former Club Bruges, Anderlecht and Sheffield Wednesday striker Marc Degryse has a stake in *Los Amigos* at Gistelsesteenweg 471, a lads' pub with disco lights and a games room. *De Platse*, on the other side at #536, is more ornate, and patronised by the older generation. The perfect mix is at *De Chalet*, #530, full of local character and host to the FC Sint-Andries pub team.

Channel tunnel and a wider range of ferries at Calais, about 1hr 15mins away on the fast (and, blissfully for France, toll-free) A16.

Getting around

The centre of Bruges is compact and you should have no use of the local buses except to get to/from the football ground or the **train station**, the latter being about 2km south-west of town – the bus station is next-door. If the sun's out, walk straight up Koning Albertlaan from the station for about 10mins and you'll arrive at Zand square, one of two pedestrian hubs of Bruges life; the other is Markt square, a further 10min walk to the right from Zand along Zuidzandstraat and Steenstraat.

There's a small tourist information desk inside the train station which can book a room for you, but the main **tourist office** (Mon–Fri 9.30am–6.30pm, Sat–Sun 10am–midday & 2–6.30pm) is on Markt square at Burg 11.

At either office you can pick up a copy of the free Flemish-language listings monthly, *Exit*.

Staying over

Bruges has plenty of small, reasonably priced hotels, but in summer they can fill up very quickly, and the situation is only going to worsen while Euro 2000 is in town. There are a number of places along Zand square, in particular **Le Singe d'Or** at 't Zand 18 (☎050/334 848, fax 050/346 628), which was a meeting place for Club Bruges players immediately before and after World War II. It has modest double rooms from 2,000BF, singles from 1,200BF, with shared bathroom facilities in the corridor. A tad more comfy is the **Hotel Jacobs** (☎050/339 831, fax 050/335 694), which has double rooms with their own bath or shower for around 2,400BF. It's less conveniently located than the Singe d'Or, but still only a 15min walk north-east from Markt. Take bus #4 or #8 from the train station, or about a 30min walk.

Few hotels in central Bruges offer car parking, so motorists could try the **Novotel Brugge Zuid**, Chartreuseweg 20 (☎050/382 581, fax 050/387 903), 4km south of town, just off the A10/E40 (exit Brugge Zuid). Double rooms go for about 3,500BF per night, but there's a garden, a heated open-air pool, and the odd barbecue with live music on the terrace.

If you want to catch a game in Bruges but the city seems full, why not stay in Ostend? The **Tulip Inn Bero Oostende**, Hofstraat 1b (☎059/702 335, fax 059/702 591), has double rooms from around 3,400BF and offers a restaurant and an indoor pool complex as well as parking in its own garage. There are dozens of other options, some of them a fair bit cheaper, in the streets around.

Eating, drinking, clubbing

Bruges is one of those small tourist towns where the nightlife is best during the week. At weekends, the cafés around Markt square are packed with coachloads of people from out of town, making those around Zand a more bearable option. Follow the locals' example and head for the little Flemish bars that seem to be tucked away down every back alley.

Between Zand and Markt at Kemelstraat 5 is **'t Brugs Beertje**, a friendly pub famous for its selection of more than 200 beers that's open 4pm–1am (closed Wed). In contrast, the excellent local Straffe Hendrik beer is the only brew on offer at the **Huisbrouwerij**, Walplein 26, a 10min walk from either Zand or the station.

For good tapas and football chatter, try **Vino Vino**, behind the theatre at Grauwwerkerstraat 15, while for more traditional Flemish fare, **Le Chagall**, just off the Markt at Sint-Ammandsstraat 40, has eel, mussels and shellfish main courses for around 500BF a throw.

The town's major venue for live acts and DJs is the **Cactus Café**, also near the Markt at Sint-Jakobsstraat 33, while **The Top**, Sint-Salvatorskerkhof 5, is a dance-music bar attracting the Cercle fraternity and anyone else interested in listening to some decent sounds until late on.

BRUSSELS

Brussels' position in European football went down several notches following the Heysel disaster of 1985. Not only was the city's reputation in tatters, it lost its popularity as a venue for European finals (it had previously hosted eight, including the European Championship final of 1972). Even the home club who once played in the stadium complex, Racing

Jet Brussels, moved out to Wavre, 30km away, in 1988. Whether the Stade Roi Baudouin that was built in Heysel's place will stage as many big matches is open to question. The 1996 Cup-Winners' Cup final between Paris St-Germain and Rapid Vienna, with its potentially explosive mix of fans, passed off without a hitch, and the authorities hope the same will be said after the Euro 2000 matches, which include the opening ceremony and inaugural fixture.

In terms of league football Brussels has always been dominated by one club – Union Saint-Gilloise before World War II, Anderlecht after it. The others folded, migrated or merged to form the city's poor relation, Racing White Daring Molenbeek, or RWDM for short. All of which leaves the Roi Baudouin as the only Euro 2000 stadium without a host club, and Anderlecht's impressive Parc Astrid as the biggest football ground in the Low Countries not being used for the finals.

As for Brussels itself, it's not the most immediately attractive of the cities playing host to Euro 2000, and its status as one of the continent's political and business capitals also makes it one of the most expensive. Yet

A king's rain – braving it under the brollies at Brussels' Roi Baudouin

there is a good, solid football town trying to get out from under all the big-city trimmings, and as a base for seeing not just matches at the Roi Baudouin but in nearby Charleroi and Bruges as well, Brussels is an appealing, commonsense choice.

Getting there

Brussels **airport** is at Zaventem, 14km north-east of town, connected by the Airport City Express train (85BF, every 20mins, 5.30am–11.30pm, journey time 20mins) to all three main train stations. Buy your ticket at the office beforehand as the inspector will ask for a hefty surcharge onboard. There is also an hourly **bus service** to the main bus station by the Gare du Nord, operating from the ground-floor level of the airport's new terminal (70BF, journey 35mins). A taxi will cost around 1,500BF.

Motorists arriving by ferry at **Ostend** have a leisurely hour and a half's drive south-east to the city along the A10/E40; add a further hour if coming from **Calais** via ferry or Le Shuttle.

Domestic mainline **trains** all call at Gare du Nord, Gare Centrale and Gare du Midi, but the **Eurostar service** from London's Waterloo International (seven departures a day, journey time 2hrs 40mins) serves Gare du Midi only.

Getting around

City **transport** is made up of three **Métro lines** – 1A, 1B (both red) and 2 (orange) – which all cross at Arts-Loi. There is also a blue **Pre-Métro** line connecting Gare du Nord and Gare du Midi; the Bourse stop is the most central, serving the city's showpiece Grand Place. A tram system also runs underground, and a network of buses overground. The whole service runs 5.30am–midnight. There is no night transport.

A single **ticket** costs 50BF, a five-journey ticket 240BF and a ten-journey one 340BF – all available from bus or tram drivers, Métro kiosks and STIB offices. A 24-hour pass is 130BF. You're trusted to validate tickets as you enter the Métro stop or bus. To enter some trams, caress the felt strip dividing the two door halves.

Taxis are rarely hailed. Pick one up outside the main train stations or order one by phone – call *Taxis Verts* on ☎02/349 4646 or *Taxi Orange* on ☎02/511 2288. Minimum charge is 95BF (plus 75BF night tariff), plus 38BF per km inside the city's 19 districts (*communes*), rising to 76BF outside.

The TIB **tourist office** in the Grand Place (open daily 9am–6pm) is cramped and over-crowded. If you're arriving at the airport, the **Destination Belgium** info desk (open daily 6.30am–9pm, ☎02/720 5161) can book accommodation for you – you pay a deposit upfront and have the amount deducted from your bill. The **Belgian Tourist Reservation Service** (☎02/513 7484, fax 02/513 9277) can do the same.

Venue verdict – the Stade Roi Baudouin

The Roi Baudouin has its own stop at the end of Métro line 1A, 20mins from Gare du Midi. This leads you out onto Avenue des Athlètes, with the main entrance around the corner on Avenue du Marathon.

For a time after the Heysel disaster, the stadium, which had been built in 1930 as part of the Parc des Expositions in north-west Brussels, was closed. Then, after much haggling over who should foot the bill for refurbishment (the national government, local authorities and the Belgian FA eventually split the cost between them), it was decided to build the Stade Roi Baudouin in its place — though some parts of the original ground, including Jozef van Neck's impressive façade, remain. The first part of the renovation was completed in 1996, the second in 1998. Today the stadium is a 50,000-capacity all-seater.

As in Charleroi and Liège, the four sectors of the Roi Baudouin are numbered. For Euro 2000, the most expensive seats occupy the whole of the main stand (sector 1) and the bulk of sector 3 opposite. There is some medium-priced accommodation at either end of sector 3, and in the four corners of sectors 2 and 4 behind each goal. The areas immediately behind the goals, which are some way from the pitch, offer the lowest-priced seating.

At the main entrance is a spacious new sports bar, *Extra-Time*, the back wall of which is plastered with shots from classic Belgium-Holland clashes. The beer served here before and during the game is alcohol-free. Facing the ground on the parallel Avenue Houba de Strooper is the friendly *Corner* bar, while at #264, 5mins towards town by the Houba-Brogmann Métro stop, is *La Coupole*, a shabbily appealing Molenbeek bar.

Some English-language listings are published by *The Bulletin* (weekly, 85BF), including film and TV information. For club and concert details, get a copy of the French-language *Kiosque* (monthly, 60BF) or the slightly less comprehensive *Bruxelscope* (28BF).

Staying over

In Brussels, as in so many other business-class cities, it all depends on whether you want to stay midweek or over a weekend. If the former, you'll find accommodation prices high and space tight. The latter, and even with Euro 2000 in town you should still be able to find a bargain.

Though the cheap hotels around Nord and Midi stations look tempting, many of them are rather seedy. Instead, take the Métro to Bourse and try the **Fouquets** at Rue de la Bourse 6 (☎02/512 0020, fax 02/512 9357), which has singles from around 1,800BF and doubles from 2,200BF; or the **George V** at Rue 't Kint 23 (☎02/513 5093, fax 02/513 4493), a period hotel where the balconies look out on to a whole mess of bars down below – singles here start around 2,200BF, doubles 2,600BF.

Near the cathedral (Métro Madou) is the **Hotel Madou** at Rue du Congrès 45 (☎02/218 8375, fax 02/217 3274), with a variety of rooms starting at 1,800BF for a single and 2,300BF a double, while a 5min walk from the Gare du Nord (Métro Rogier) is the more upmarket **Hotel des Colonies**, Rue des Croisades 6–10 (☎02/203 3094, fax 02/203 2944), one of the oldest three-star hotels in Brussels, with newly renovated singles at 2,000–3,950BF, doubles at 2,200–4,800BF, depending on dates.

Eating, drinking, clubbing

Brussels has neither the hip cachet of Amsterdam nor the fashionable trappings of Paris, but in a lot of ways it's more fun than either. Unpretentious bars full of locals abound, even just a few minutes' walk from the bright lights of the Grand Place, and the city's international feel means there's a massive range of restaurant cuisines on offer.

The most famous bar in all Brussels is **à la Mort Subite** at Rue Montagne aux Herbes Portagères 7 (Métro to De Brouckère), which serves the eponymous 'Sudden Death' beer and has hardly changed since the 1920s. In the same area, **Kafka**, Rue de la Vierge Noire 6, offers a choice of 50 beers, 18 different vodkas, or a cup of hot Oxo.

Another well-known establishment is **Le Falstaff**, Rue Henri Maus 19–25 (Métro Bourse), an *art nouveau* café/restaurant serving large portions of main courses until 3am Mon–Fri, 5am Sat–Sun, with *plats du jour* at under 500BF. Nearby but more touristy is **Chez Léon**, Rue des Bouchers 18, which packs them in with cheap plates of mussels and a set menu at 395BF – there's another branch up at the Roi Baudouin.

Also in the vicinity of Bourse is **l'Archiduc**, Rue Antoine Dansaert 6, a jazz club done out like something from a Fred Astaire movie, with live music and civilised opening hours of 4pm–4am. First and still the best techno club in town is **The Fuse**, Rue Blaes 208, open Sats only with top-name DJs spinning until 7.30am; Métro to Porte de Hal.

CHARLEROI

The Charleroi area is the biggest conurbation in Wallonia, the French-speaking half of Belgium, and has been a centre of heavy industry for generations. Like the city of Lens at the 1998 World Cup, it seems an unlikely host venue for a major international football event but, also like Lens, it hopes to shake off its underdog image and prove itself as the model of what a football town should be: compact, friendly, unpretentious and true to its roots.

Central Charleroi is indeed compact – perhaps a little too much so, with few amenities for the expected rush of fans from across the continent, and a number of security concerns as a result. And, unlike Lens, the town has no great domestic footballing tradition. The biggest local side, Royal Charleroi Sporting Club (known in these parts as 'Sporting'), have nothing more than a couple of losing appearances in cup finals to their name, and prior to this year their Mambourg stadium had played host to just two internationals in 50 years.

Still, Charleroi does offer a taste of the authentic Low Countries football experience, a world away from the brash arenas of Brussels and Amsterdam, where a few thousand hardy souls brave all weathers to follow the fortunes of *les Zèbres*, and where the air is thick with the smell of frying chips, cheap cigar smoke and cheerful irony.

Sandwiched – Charleroi's triple-decker, as seen through the players' tunnel

Getting there

Three **trains** an hour leave from Brussels Nord for Charleroi Sud, calling at Brussels Central and Midi along the way (total journey time 45mins). Charleroi Sud is also served by two trains an hour from Liège Guillemins (journey 1hr 20mins). For connections to other cities in Belgium and Holland, change at Brussels Midi.

Motorists arriving at **Ostend** should take the A10/E40 south-east as far as Brussels, then the A7/E19 off the southern ring road to Nivelles, and the A54 from there to Charleroi. Coming from Calais, take the A16/E40 east as far as Dunkerque, then the A25/E42 south toward Lille. Follow this road past Lille to Mons and then Charleroi – its local 'A' number changes as you drive from France into Belgium, but it retains its European E42 designation all the way to Charleroi.

Coming from either direction, you need allow no more than 2hrs 30mins for the mainland Europe part of the car journey. Note also that all the roads mentioned above are toll-free, even in France.

Getting around

Central Charleroi can be divided into two areas: the lower town, where you'll arrive at the Gare du Sud if coming by train; and the upper town, hub of the city's commercial life, which you must pass through in order to get to the stadium.

During the day, regular TEC red-and-yellow minibuses make the 5min journey from the Gare du Sud to the Place du Manège in the upper town, or you can take the metro from Sud to Beaux Arts. However, Charleroi's municipal transport tends to give up the ghost early and, given that all three Euro 2000 games scheduled to be played here kick-off at 8.45pm, the authorities will be laying on shuttle buses to take fans between the stadium, the upper town and the Gare du Sud.

The local **tourist office** (Mon–Fri 8.30am–midday & 1–5pm) is opposite the Gare du Sud.

Staying over

As an industrial town, Charleroi is ill-equipped to deal with significant numbers of tourists, and hotel accommodation of all kinds is thin on the ground here. In the expectation that almost anything worth having will be booked in advance, it might make more sense to stay in Brussels, where there is more chance of getting a room on-spec.

If you must stay locally, **Pim's Hotel**, just across the square from the Gare du Sud at Place E Buisset 13 (☎071/319 870, fax 071/334 440), has around 30 rooms, with singles from 2,200BF and doubles from 2,600BF. Also near the station at Boulevard Mayence 1a is the **Holiday Inn Garden Court** (☎071/302 424, fax 071/304 949), with the expected high standard of decor and doubles from 3,750BF. Towards the upper town at Boulevard J Tirou 96 is the **Socatel** (☎071/319 811, fax 071/301 596), with its own restaurant and car parking, and rooms from 2,550BF.

If you're travelling by car, another option might be to stay on the outskirts of Charleroi, making use of the shuttle buses which are due to ferry supporters between a series of out-of-town car parks and the stadium (see panel).

The **Motel Nivelles-Sud** at Chausée de Mons 22 (☎067/218 721, fax 067/221 088) is just off the A54 motorway between Nivelles and Charleroi and offers free parking, its own restaurant and an outdoor pool among

other amenities. Double rooms here are priced from 5,000BF, singles
from 4,500BF.

Eating, drinking, clubbing

Nowhere does the prospect of a Euro 2000 alcohol ban loom larger than
in Charleroi, and the following venues may be alcohol-free (or indeed
closed altogether) before, during and after local matchdays.

Most of the city's nightlife is centred around Place du Manège in the
upper town. Here you'll find a string of agreeable bars, among which **Les
Templiers** also offers a good-value menu. Among the other food options
on the square are Greek cooking at **Athenes** at #19, and Italian at the
Imperial right next-door.

Venue verdict – the Stade du Pays de Charleroi

Though it has been renamed after the regional council which assisted with its refurbishment, most locals still refer to the ground by its former name of 'Le Mambourg'.
It's on Boulevard Zoé Drion, off Boulevard Dewandre in the northern part of Charleroi's
upper town, and the easiest way to get to it will be via shuttle bus – either from
the Gare du Sud in the lower town, or from a number of out-of-town car parks
which are being specially designated for Euro 2000 and will be clearly signposted
along the E42 motorway and the southern section of the city's ring road.

Before work began on transforming Le Mambourg for the tournament, it had a
capacity of only 10,000. Today it has a capacity of 30,000, but there's a catch – the
top level of seating in the three-tier, Tribune 3, opposite the main stand, is only temporary. After the tournament, this level will be removed and the roof lowered so that
it is the same height as those over Tribunes 2 and 4 behind the goals. The distinctive
pyramid-shaped design of Tribune 3 has been criticised by local police, who worry
that it is too steep. The architects retort that, with an incline of 37°, it is at a shal-
lower angle than equivalent tiers of seating at the San Siro in Milan.

For Euro 2000, the most expensive seats occupy most of Tribune 1 and the central sections of all three tiers in Tribune 3, with medium-priced seating available in
the upper tiers of Tribunes 2 and 4 and at either end of Tribune 3, and cheapest
category places at the front of 2 and 4, as well as at the far ends of Tribune 1.

On Place Charles II, a 2min walk south-east from Place du Manège along Rue du Dauphin, there's **Le Napoléon** offering decent Belgian grub and a wide range of beers with which to wash it down, and the slightly more upmarket **Gourmets d'Asie**.

The **Palais des Beaux Arts**, part of Charleroi's Palais des Expositions on Avenue de l'Europe behind Place du Manège, attracts most of the major live acts touring Belgium and also stages gigs by local bands. Those seeking club or DJ action are probably better off in Brussels.

EINDHOVEN

Eindhoven is a peculiar town. It is home to Holland's third most successful football team and the huge Philips industrial and research plant that finances it – and little else. Nearly one in five people are employed by the electrical conglomerate and many of these are regulars at the football club.

PSV are the richest team in Holland and have a stadium to match. For Philips, this expense is an investment – the chance to send the company name around the globe. In any case, PSV is a profit centre in its own right, the club's management having made a serious surplus from the sale of players like Ruud Gullit, Ronald Koeman, Romário and Ronaldo. The club's enormous financial clout also means that the team are the most unpopular in Holland. Ajax and Feyenoord may hate each other, but everyone hates PSV.

The stadium is a short walk from the train station, so many Euro 2000 visits may be of the flying variety. But if you do choose to stay, Eindhoven's affluent youth has generated a surprisingly chic and animated nightlife – some recompense for the lack of any other sights in the town.

Getting there

Two **trains** an hour leave from Amsterdam Centraal for Eindhoven (direction Maastricht, journey time 1hr 10mins), and the same frequency applies for services from Rotterdam (journey 1hr 20mins, most trains originate in The Hague). If you're coming from Belgium, you can catch one of the hourly trains from Liège to Maastricht and change there for Eindhoven (total journey 1hr 45mins).

Motorists arriving at the **Hook of Holland** should take the A15/E31 east past Rotterdam as far as the junction with the A2/E25, then the latter road south to Eindhoven – allow a couple of hours.

Eindhoven has a small **airport** 6km west of the centre, connected to the train station by bus #8 (7.30am–6pm, journey time 30mins). It's more likely, though, that you'll arrive at Amsterdam's Schipol if flying – almost all the Eindhoven trains mentioned above call at the airport before moving on to Amsterdam Centraal.

Getting around

Eindhoven is part of Holland's *treintaxi* scheme, whereby rail travellers who have paid an extra f7 can take a taxi anywhere in town for free when they get to their destination. Otherwise the station is a 5min walk from the centre of town, much of which is pedestrianised. A network of **city buses** runs 7am–11pm, with fares operating on the *Strippenkaart* system. The main routes run after midnight Fri–Sat.

Public relations – the lighting always looks good at the Philips Stadion

Eindhoven's **tourist office** is right outside the train station. Here you'll find the Dutch-language **listings** publication, *Uit-CultuurKrant*.

Staying over

Much of Eindhoven's hotel accommodation is geared toward business travellers (and priced to match), but there's also a fair sprinkling of smaller hotels and pensions – book in advance if you can. Of the latter, the **Corso** at Vestdijk 17 (☎040/244 9131) is on the main drag that runs from the train

Venue verdict – the Philips Stadion

You could take a bus (#12, #13 or #14), but in the time it takes for one to come along, you'd probably have walked the quarter of a mile from Eindhoven train station to the stadium – simply turn right as you exit the station and keep going straight down Mathildelaan.

Until the renovation of de Kuip in 1994 and the construction of the Amsterdam Arena, the Philips Stadion was the best in Holland. It still is a very comfortable place in which to see a football match, with superb facilities for the business crowd and rooftop gas heaters warming everyone else down below in winter. Walking around the stadium – the ground level is dominated by a huge *Toys R Us* store – reveals four floors of business lounges and sponsors' restaurants.

The latest innovation, at a ground which is constantly being upgraded to showcase the technological progress being made by its corporate owners, is the provision of four giant TV screens so that wherever you sit in the stadium, you can see instant replays of the action.

For Euro 2000, the most expensive seats take up most of the Noord stand (entrance in Mathildelaan) and the Zuid stand opposite, while there is medium-category seating in the upper tiers of the Oost and West stands behind the goals, as well as in all four corners of the stadium. The cheapest seats are in the lower tiers of the Oost and West stands.

For a pre-match swiftie, the younger element head for *D'N Berk*, on the corner of Gagelstraat and Mathildelaan, a minute's walk from the stadium. There'll be a couple of bouncers on the door, loud music from the DJ and, assuming there's no alcohol ban, a crowd three deep at the bar. A more comfortable supporters' bar is accessible through gate #12 of the stadium, as is a PSV souvenir shop.

station through town; it has singles, doubles and triples at around f70, f100 and f140 respectively. Also offering modest accommodation is the **Oud Eindhoven** at Stratumseind 63 (☎040/244 4559), which is perfectly located if you're living it up, but could be annoyingly noisy if not; singles and doubles from around f90.

Among the more upmarket choices, the **Tulip Inn** couldn't be more centrally located at Markt 35 (☎040/245 4545, fax 040/243 5645). As well as double rooms in the f150–250 bracket, it has two restaurants and is directly opposite a mall with over 100 shops (and a 24-hour car park). Motorists have the additional option of the **Novotel Eindhoven** at Anthony Fokkerweg 101 (☎040/252 6575, fax 040/252 2850), next to the Eindhoven airport exit off the A2/E25 motorway. Double rooms here aren't cheap at f275 per night, but the parking is free and the city centre is only a 10min drive away.

Eating, drinking, clubbing

A close-knit network of city-centre streets including Kleine Berg and Stratumseind is where you'll find Eindhoven's nightlife. All the main venues are within an easy walk of each other and, in turn, to/from the train station. **Baloo's Blues** at Kleine Berg 60 is an accessible rockers' pub with a pool table, loud music and Baloo the Bear memorabilia, while the **Grand Café Berlage**, at #16 in the same street, has a summer terrace plus two side bars where you can eat cheaply as well as drink.

For a serious meal try **Ajdanski**, Stratumseind 81, which is run by former PSV player Petar Ajdanski and offers special deals on Balkan dishes Mon–Thur. **Touch Of India**, Geldropseweg 22, is the city's only Indian restaurant and offers special buffet deals for around f40 – it's open evenings only.

Just across from the train station you'll find two worthwhile music venues: **de Dans Salon** at Stationsplein 4 is Eindhoven's main disco and offers free admission before 11pm, while **Effenaar**, Dommelstraat 2, is a left-field cultural centre which might be putting on anything from Belgian hardcore to live R&B.

LIÈGE

Liège is a big, sprawling city which gives the impression of having once been much more prosperous than it presently is. Like Charleroi, it grew rich on the back of the industrial revolution and, now that the old heavy industries like coal and steel are in decline, the town has a slightly melancholic air.

Unlike Charleroi, however, this is a serious football city, proud of its place in the history of the game in Belgium and boasting, in Royal Standard de Liège, perhaps the most passionately supported club in the country. Sadly, the city's footballing fortunes have declined in tandem with its industry, the rot beginning to set in after it was discovered that Standard's seventh Belgian championship win in 1982 came courtesy of a match-fixing syndicate.

There has been trouble in the air here ever since – not least when Standard's one-time city rivals from the northern suburb of Rocourt, RC Liégeois, were forced to merge with an out-of-town club, Tilleur, to guarantee their survival in 1995; and when Standard themselves absorbed RFC Seraing, who once played just across the river Meuse from Standard's Sclessin stadium, a year later.

Standard are now on a firm financial footing thanks to the sponsorship of the Sergio Cragnotti food empire which also bankrolls Italy's Lazio. The club also, thanks to Euro 2000 refurbishments, has a massively improved stadium – a modern but still atmospheric ground, well-matched to the patient dedication and typical Walloon warmth of the team's local fan base.

Getting there

Liège has its own **airport**, Bierset, 15km west of town and connected to the centre by shuttle bus. If you want to fly, though, it'll almost certainly be cheaper to arrive at Brussels and catch a train from there. **Trains** leave from Brussels Midi twice an hour (journey time 1hr 20mins), arriving at Liège's main station, Guillemins, about 2km south of the centre. Many of the Brussels trains originate on the coast, calling first at Bruges – add 1hr to the journey if travelling from here. If you're coming to Liège from Holland, you'll need to change trains at Maastricht before heading south into Belgium.

Motorists arriving by ferry at **Ostend** should take the A10/E40 south-east as far as Brussels, circling the city using the northern half of its ring road, then the A3/E40 to Liège (in Flemish-speaking Belgium, the name to look for on road signs is 'Luik'). If coming from **Calais**, take the A16/E40 east as far as Dunkerque, then the A25/E42 south past Lille, Mons, Charleroi and Namur – its local 'A' number changes, but it retains its European E42 designation all the way to Liège.

Venue verdict – the Stade du Sclessin

The suburb of Sclessin has its own train station, used only by local trains but no more than a 5min ride south-west from Guillemins. From here it's a 5min walk to the stadium. Alternatively, bus #27 (direction Jemeppe) runs from Guillemins to Sclessin station, then calls right outside the ground – you need to get off two stops after Sclessin station, at the stop marked 'Standard'. At the bus station outside Guillemins, avoid the temptation to board bus #20 with 'Sclessin' on its front – this takes a very circuitous route and does not stop particularly close to the stadium.

The Standard club began renovating Sclessin in 1984, but much of what you'll see now dates from the 1990s, during which around three-quarters of the ground was rebuilt to produce an all-seat capacity of 30,000. The designers have kept the stands deliberately close to the pitch in an imitation of the 'English style', which helps the matchday atmosphere but also means that the top third tier is vertiginously steep.

As is the custom in French-speaking Belgium, the four sides of the stadium are numbered. Most of the main west stand (Tribune 1) and all of the two-tier east stand (Tribune 2) is made up of highest-priced seating for Euro 2000, while mid-price seating curves around from Tribune 1 into the top levels of the north stand (Tribune 3, the slagheap end) and the all-new south stand (Tribune 4, the river end). The lower two levels of the two end stands mainly comprise lowest-priced accommodation.

All four sides of the ground are now covered and, in contrast to Charleroi, the extra layers of seating provided for Euro 2000 are a permanent fixture, not a quick fix.

The area around Sclessin is not exactly a bar-hopper's paradise, but both main stands have bar areas behind their business lounges. Alternatively, have a drink in the Place des Guillemins before boarding the bus to the ground.

Under reconstruction – Sclessin has been massively rebuilt for Euro 2000

Getting around

Liège is big – the central 'new town' area around Place St-Lambert is a good 20–25mins hike up from the **Gare du Guillemins**, while the 'old town' on the hill above is even further. Local trains run to the more centrally located stations of Palais and Jonfosse, but it might be easier to use the efficient **TEC bus network**, which has a flat fare of 45BF within the city limits – pay the driver. To get quickly from Guillemins to the centre, take bus #1 or #4 to St-Lambert. **Taxis** charge 100BF per kilometre, with the usual supplements for baggage and night service.

There's a tourist **information desk** at Guillemins station (Mon–Sat 10am–4pm) but the main **tourist office** is up in the old town at Feronstrée 92 (Mon–Fri 9am–6pm, Sat 10am–4pm, Sun 10am–2pm). The former is fine for transport enquiries, while the latter is a better bet when it comes to booking accommodation.

Staying over

For such a major conurbation, Liège is surprisingly short on hotel rooms, inexpensive or otherwise. There's a fair collection of affordable places in the immediate vicinity of Guillemins station, among them the **Hotel du Midi** at Place des Guillemins 1 (☎04/252 2004), which has a couple of dozen rooms from 1,600BF and the slightly more upmarket **Hotel de la Couronne** at #11 (☎04/252 2168, fax 04/355 5552), with singles at around 2,200BF, doubles around 3,000BF. If both these are full, try the **Comfort Inn Univers** on the corner at #116 (☎04/252 2650, fax 04/252 1653) which charges broadly the same money as the Couronne and usefully has its own car park.

If you want to stay closer to Liège centre, try **Le Cygne d'Argent** at Rue Beeckman 49 (☎04/223 7001, fax 04/222 4966) which has singles at around 2,000BF, doubles for 2,600BF and a fairly priced restaurant. For a riverside location, there's the **Bedford Hotel Liège** at Quai Saint Léonard 36 (☎04/228 8111, fax 04/227 4575) where you'll pay anything up to 7,450BF for a single, 8,450BF a double, but the rooms are spacious and there are plenty of them.

Eating, drinking, clubbing

If your stomach's rumbling, Liège offers the perfect antidote – the usual vast range of Belgian beers, better wine than you'll typically get in Flanders and the best local cuisine in the country, all served up with genuine hospitality at reasonable prices.

Deciding where to go is a matter of the time of day. For lunch, the area around the Place de la République Française and the theatre in the new town is overrun with cafés offering tempting *plats du jour* for as little as 200BF. **Au Point du Vue**, on the square itself, claims to be the oldest tavern in Liège and exudes typical appeal, though it can get very crowded.

For dinner, cross the river to the atmospheric island of Outremeuse where narrow Rue Roture is a riot of lively bars and restaurants. **Pizzeria Comedia** at #38 does fine pizzas, **Les Notes en Bulles** at #41 offers more typical local cuisine, and **Acropolis** has filling Greek platters – all three charge 400BF or less for a main course.

For late-night bar-hopping and clubbing, head back across the river to the old town area of Rue Pont d'Avroy with its designer bars. The side streets are dotted with hip venues where you can catch up on Belgium's contribution to European techno – try **L'Aquarelle** on the corner of Rue de Pot d'Or and Rue Tête du Boeuf, or L'Escalier on Rue St-Jean-en-Ile.

ROTTERDAM

The football passions burning in Rotterdam are simply explained. While Amsterdam dreams, Rotterdam works – that's how the Rotterdammers see it. And that's how they see the football, too. Honest, workmanlike Feyenoord against flashy, arrogant Ajax.

Getting one over on Amsterdam has been the priority ever since the city's main stadium was opened in 1937. A favourite with UEFA for staging European finals, *'de Kuip'* ('The Tub') has seen a lot of classic football in a fervent atmosphere. But by the end of the 1980s it was falling to pieces, and Rotterdam city council had to step in to give it a complete overhaul, putting up the Maas building for VIPs and sponsors, and making the site more attractive to the business community.

Yet the surrounding Feijenoord area, unlike so much of Amsterdam, still feels like it belongs to the game, its rundown bars embellished with tatty pictures of its beloved soccer-playing stars. This is a football patch *par excellence*, a rare part of Holland where you feel as if football, and doubtless much more, is still being practised in the street.

Getting there

Bus #33 runs from Rotterdam's small **airport** into town, but since flights are much cheaper to Amsterdam, many visitors arrive via **Schipol**, which is connected to **Rotterdam Centraal station** by an hourly train service (journey time 1hr). Centraal is a short walk from Rotterdam's imposing modern centre. Motorists arriving at the **Hook of Holland** have no more than a 20min drive into central Rotterdam via the A20/E25.

Getting around

Rotterdam's **city transport** consists of buses, trams and metro, run on Holland's universal *Strippenkaart* system – two bars will take you to anywhere central. There is an extensive night bus network at weekends; tickets are f5 and all routes call at either Centraal station or Zuidplein, where **taxis** should be available. If not, simply phone ☎010/462 6060.

The **tourist office** (☎010/402 3234, fax 010/413 0124) is a 10min walk from Centraal station at Coolsingel 67.

For **listings information**, the monthly *R'uit* (f2.50) offers tips on both high- and low-brow culture.

Staying over

As Holland's second-largest city and the country's biggest port, Rotterdam has no shortage of accommodation, particularly at the cheaper end. These are not concentrated in any one particular area, however, and some can be on the seedy side. If you're turning up on-spec, it might be an idea to use the accommodation booking service offered by the **tourist office** (see above), which charges only a very modest commission.

Venue verdict – the Stadion Feyenoord

On Euro 2000 matchdays a special train service, the *Voetbaltrein*, will run every 20mins from Centraal station to Stadion, opposite the ground – about a 10min journey. There are strict controls at the gate, so be sure to stamp your *Strippenkaart* on the third bar. If you miss the train, bus #49 also runs from outside Centraal to Olympiaweg.

One of the best-loved footballing arenas in mainland Europe, 'de Kuip' has been gradually extended and modernised over the years without losing its frenetic atmosphere. It now holds 50,000 all-seated, with the latest improvement being additional roofing which means that 80% of those spectators now have protection against the elements. Hooliganism has continued to be a problem here, however, and while the perimeter fencing has gone, the moat between the stands and the field of play is there for a reason.

The three Euro 2000 ticketing categories are straightforwardly arranged, with almost the whole of the two side sectors, the Maastribune and the Olympiatribune, comprising highest-priced seating; medium-priced seating in all four corners of the ground and in the pitch-level stands along both sides; and the cheapest seats in the Stadiontribune and Marathontribune at each end, as well as at pitch level in front of them.

Many bars just across the river have the atmosphere of old Feijenoord. One, on the corner of Roetgenstraat and Oranjeboomstraat by the first #49 bus stop over the bridge from town, is actually called *Café Oud Feijenoord*. Nearer the stadium, on the #77 bus route towards it, is the *Café Schuyer* on the corner of Slaghekstraat and Beijerlandse. The best of the lot is *Café Boulevard Zuid* nearby, where Laantjesweg and Beijerlandse meet – pin-ups of Feyenoord's old stars line the counter.

A short walk north of Centraal station is **Hotel Bienvenue**, Spoorsingel 24 (☎010/466 9394, fax 010/467 7475), an excellent-value place with singles at around f75 without bath/shower, f80 with, and some doubles also available. A little further afield, **Hotel Wilgenhof**, Heemradsingel 92–94 (☎010/425 4892, fax 010/477 2611), is a medium-sized, comfortable three-star hotel with 80 rooms and a restaurant downstairs. Singles here are around f95 without bath/shower, f125 with – take tram #4 from Centraal station.

The **Astoria**, Pleinweg 203–205 (☎010/485 6634, fax 010/485 4602), is a one-star, no-nonsense joint the other side of the river near the Maastunnel. It has a late bar, a TV room with a massive screen and, reportedly, a former Miss World serving

True to its roots – Feyenoord's 'tub'

breakfast. Singles here are around f65, doubles f110 – take tram #2 from Maashaven metro.

More upmarket and centrally located is the **Savoy**, Hoogstraat 81 (☎010/413 9280, fax 010/404 5712), with singles in the 165–270BF range, doubles 180–310BF, and car parking in a garage next-door.

Eating, drinking, clubbing

Without the tourists, there is a sharper, more determined pace to nightlife in Rotterdam than in Amsterdam. Early evening, the harbour area between Blaak and Willems bridge, Oudehaven, is ideal for a quiet pils. By night, the streets Nieuwe Binnenweg and Witte de Withstraat, either side of

Eendrachtsplein metro stop, are packed with bars; the former is rather seedy at one end, while the latter attracts an artier crowd.

If you want an afternoon in the heart of Feijenoord, **Café t'Haantje**, Bierens de Haanweg 12, is for you. Former Feyenoord coach Ernst Happel spent many a card session here with his players in the 1970s, and there's a full menu on offer – take bus #47 or #48 from Zuidplein metro to Spinozaweg. A more mainstream sports café is **Schieland**, Schiekade 770, with Feyenoord memorabilia and a giant TV screen – tram #3 or #5 from Centraal station.

Cosmopolitan Rotterdam has a wide range of dining options. Cheap lunchtime sitdowns can be found around the Lijnbaan shopping centre, but you may not need to go that far. **Restaurant Engels**, Stationsplein 45, is a bizarre multi-restaurant setup opposite Centraal station, with Tokaj (Hungarian), Beefeater (English), Don Quijote (Spanish) and Engels Brasserie all in one place; it's a tad pricy, but convenient. **Midnight**, 1e Middellandstraat 57b, is a late-night, early-morning diner within walking distance of the city's main bar areas, open until 4am Sun–Thurs, 6am Fri–Sat – tram #1, #7 or #9 from Centraal station.

Rotterdam is a good clubbers' city, too. Within a 5min walk from Centraal station is **Nighttown** at West-Kruiskade 28, a varied disco and concert venue, while next-door is the **Café Popular** with jazz and underground music concerts. A little further afield is **Rotown**, Nieuwe Binnenweg 19, a multi-purpose restaurant and live music venue in an old Rotterdam townhouse, surrounded by late-night bars and open until 2am, 3am weekends – tram #4 from Centraal station.

MATCH SCHEDULE

Date	Time (local/UK)	Venue	Fixture	Group
10 June	8.45pm/7.45pm	Brussels	Belgium—Sweden	B
11 June	2.30pm/1.30pm	Arnhem	Turkey—Italy	B
	6.00pm/5.00pm	Bruges	France—Denmark	D
	8.45pm/7.45pm	Amsterdam	Holland—Czech Rep	D
12 June	6.00pm/5.00pm	Liège	Germany—Romania	A
	8.45pm/7.45pm	Eindhoven	Portugal—England	A
13 June	6.00pm/5.00pm	Rotterdam	Spain—Norway	C
	8.45pm/7.45pm	Charleroi	Yugoslavia—Slovenia	C
14 June	8.45pm/7.45pm	Brussels	Italy—Belgium	B
15 June	8.45pm/7.45pm	Eindhoven	Sweden—Turkey	B
16 June	6.00pm/5.00pm	Bruges	Czech Rep—France	D
	8.45pm/7.45pm	Rotterdam	Denmark—Holland	D
17 June	6.00pm/5.00pm	Arnhem	Romania—Portugal	A
	8.45pm/7.45pm	Charleroi	England—Germany	A
18 June	6.00pm/5.00pm	Amsterdam	Slovenia—Spain	C
	8.45pm/7.45pm	Liège	Norway—Yugoslavia	C
19 June	8.45pm/7.45pm	Brussels	Turkey—Belgium	B
	8.45pm/7.45pm	Eindhoven	Italy—Sweden	B
20 June	8.45pm/7.45pm	Charleroi	England—Romania	A
	8.45pm/7.45pm	Rotterdam	Portugal—Germany	A
21 June	6.00pm/5.00pm	Bruges	Yugoslavia—Spain	C
	6.00pm/5.00pm	Arnhem	Slovenia—Norway	C
	8.45pm/7.45pm	Liège	Denmark—Czech Rep	D
	8.45pm/7.45pm	Amsterdam	France—Holland	D

Quarter-finals

Date	Time (local/UK)	Venue	Fixture
24 June	6.00pm/5.00pm	Amsterdam	Match 25: B2—A1
	8.45pm/7.45pm	Brussels	Match 26: B1—A2
25 June	6.00pm/5.00pm	Rotterdam	Match 27: D1—C2
	8.45pm/7.45pm	Bruges	Match 28: C1—D2

Semi-finals

Date	Time (local/UK)	Venue	Fixture
28 June	8.45pm/7.45pm	Brussels	Match 29: winner 28—winner 25
29 June	6.00pm/5.00pm	Amsterdam	Match 30: winner 26—winner 27

Final

Date	Time (local/UK)	Venue	Fixture
2 July	8.00pm/7.00pm	Rotterdam	Match 31: winner 29—winner 30

TOURNAMENT HISTORY

1958–60

After a Frenchman, **Henri Delaunay**, first proposes the idea of a European Championship in the mid-1950s, the inaugural competition kicks off on 5 April 1958. The event is initially known as the **European Nations' Cup**. Delaunay dies before the tournament gets underway and the trophy is named after him. Despite the established appeal of the World Cup, some FAs are sceptical and **absentees** from the first event include Italy, West Germany and all four 'home' nations. The tournament's **final stages** (semi-finals onwards) are hosted by the French, who surprisingly lose their semi 5–4 to Yugoslavia, who in turn are beaten 2–1 by the **Soviet Union** after extra time in the final.

1962–64

All the home nations except Scotland are persuaded to enter but the tournament is still a relatively **lightweight affair**, with a straight knockout format rather than qualifying groups. Among the odder results are **Luxembourg**'s defeat of Holland and Albania's walk over Greece, who refused to play them for political reasons. Holders the Soviet Union again progress all the way to the final, but this time they are beaten 2–1 by **Spain** in Madrid, in front of General Franco who had refused his side permission to travel to the USSR four years earlier.

1966–68

Qualifying groups are used for the first time as the tournament **continues to expand**. World Cup holders England make their best progress to date, losing to Yugoslavia in the semi-finals after being reduced to ten men. The Yugoslavs then lose a replayed final to hosts **Italy** after the latter are awarded a controversial free-kick equaliser in the first game. The Italians had earlier had their semi-final against the Soviet Union decided on the **toss of a coin**.

1970–72

West Germany sweep all before them in what is only the second European Championship they have entered. **England** are beaten 3–1 at Wembley in the quarter-finals, to be followed in the semis by Belgium (who host the final stages) and by the Soviet Union in the final, 3–0. The **Germans' domination** is a foretaste of what is to come at the 1974 World Cup, which the team of Beckenbauer, Breitner, Müller and company also goes on to win in style.

1974–76

The last finals to consist **solely of knockout games** are widely considered to be a classic of their era. All four matches go to extra time and no team fails to score in any game as the **'total football'** of Holland and West Germany comes up against the canny counter-attacking of **Czechoslovakia** and hosts **Yugoslavia**. The Dutch are surprisingly beaten by the Czechs in their semi after being reduced to nine men, while the Germans come back from 2–0 down to eliminate the hosts with **typical resilience**. In the final, West Germany claw back another two-goal deficit but cannot quite finish the job against **Czechoslovakia**, who win the subsequent **penalty shoot-out.**

1978–80

The Italians play host as UEFA expands the final stages to **eight teams**, arranged in two groups of four. Clumsily, however, the competition is given no semi-final stage, meaning that the two group winners go straight through to the final. The arrangement **frustrates good football** and infuriates fans, contributing to the worst scenes of **hooliganism** yet seen at a European Championship. **Police use teargas** as England are held 1–1 by Belgium, who proceed to the final and narrow defeat by **West Germany**, who win 2–1 in the dying seconds.

1982–84

The finals are belatedly given a **decent structure** and France, Portugal, Spain and Denmark qualify for the semi-finals from the eight-team group stage. Spain edge Denmark on penalties while hosts France beat Portugal 3–2 in a game often referred to as **the finest** the competition has seen. The final doesn't live up to it, the French needing a goal-keeping blunder to set them on the way to a 2–1 win, but victory is well-deserved by Platini and the **fluid footballing side** he captains.

1986–88

After missing out on Euro '84, England return to the finals in West Germany and are **immediately ousted** by Ireland, Holland and the Soviet Union. The Dutch then beat the Irish and, in the semi-finals, a dumbstruck host nation to set up a final against the Soviets. Holland had lost the group encounter between the two, but **Rijkaard, van Basten and Gullit** hit their stride in the final in Munich and win comfortably, 2–0.

1990–92

The 'friendly finals' are again blighted by hooliganism but the enduring memory for England fans is **Graham Taylor** substituting Gary Lineker before the end of his side's last-game defeat (and elimination) by hosts Sweden. The Swedes then lose their semi-final to the first **united Germany team** to take part in an international finals, but attention then switches to the other semi where holders Holland are surprisingly beaten on penalties by Denmark. The Danes are only in the finals because Yugoslavia have been **expelled** a week before the tournament is due to commence, yet their 'nothing to lose' attitude then carries them past Germany in the final, amid cries of 'Auf Wiedersehen' from Denmark's disbelieving supporters.

1994–96

England host the finals for the first time and the event, **newly expanded** to 16 teams arranged in four groups of four, is widely judged a success. The hosts' progress includes an emotional 2–0 win over Scotland and a 4–1 thrashing of Holland, and *Football's Coming Home* sweeps the country. Terry Venables' side **seems unstoppable** but the Germans have other ideas, beating England on penalties in the semi-finals before edging the Czech Republic out of the final with a **'golden goal'** from Oliver Bierhoff.